MUNICH

CONTENTS

46

Top 10 of Everything

76

Area by Area

136

Streetsmart

MUNICH

INTRODUCING

Englischer Garten

WELCOME TO
MUNICH

RA fascinating blend of high-tech innovation and unique historic traditions, Munich is a city that rewards exploration beyond stereotypes of beer and Lederhosen. Don't want to miss a thing? With Top 10 Munich, you'll enjoy the very best the city has to offer.

Fondly referred to as "the village with a million inhabitants", modern metropolis Munich has a unique small-town charm. A stroll through its medieval heart is like walking into a fairy-tale village, with cobblestone lanes, picturesque plazas and the many historical buildings around

Marienplatz showcasing just about every major architectural style, from the Romanesque and Gothic to the Renaissance and Baroque. But look beyond these picture book good looks and you'll discover a cultural powerhouse: Munich is home to world-class art and culture with over

Diners at Hofbräuhaus

50 galleries and museums in the Museum Quarter alone. Explore cutting-edge science and technology at the Deutsches Museum or see works by artistic masters, both historic and contemporary, at the Pinakothek galleries. Meanwhile the futuristic designs of the BMW Welt and ceramic rod- covered Museum Brandhorst show just how much the city continues to reinvent itself.

Munich frequently tops the charts for its art, culture and history, but this is a place that knows how to have fun, too. This is never more clear than during Oktoberfest, the city's world-famous annual festival, though you'll find a celebratory energy pervades almost everything, at any time of year: the hearty food, traditional beer halls, raucous night life scene and even the city's 5,000 acres of green space. Here you'll find surfers plying the Eisbach's waves, families and friends sharing happy moments, and an abundance of beer gardens, of course. There's little more joyful than a rousing cry of "Prost!" at the end of a day exploring this dynamic city.

So, where to start? With Top 10 Munich, of course. This pocket-sized guide gets to the heart of the city with simple lists of 10, expert local knowledge and comprehensive maps, helping you turn an ordinary trip into an extraordinary one.

THE STORY OF
MUNICH

Since its foundation in 1158, Munich has endured everything from hardship and occupations to periods of magnificent success and expansion, mostly under the 700-year rule of the Wittelsbach dynasty, who shaped and moulded the city. Here's the story of how it came to be.

Early Settlers

Though settlements around Bavaria date back to the 4th millennium BCE, the word "Munich" does not appear in the historical record until the 12th century CE. The first settlers in the fertile region around modern-day Munich were Celts, who arrived in the first millennium BCE. Around 15 BCE, the Romans conquered the region, up to the Danube, and the following centuries were dominated by first the Romans, and then Germanic peoples. Historians believe that Munich itself can only trace its history back to a Benedictine monastery built here in the 8th century – the name Munich (or München) means "home of the monks". Even so, it wasn't until 1157 that Henry the Lion, Duke of Bavaria, granted the monks the right to establish a market and built a bridge across the Isar river, all in an attempt to control the salt trade. A year later, the word Munich appeared in documents, and by 1175, the settlement had swelled to 2,500 and was encircled by a stone wall. Thus, it was formally recognized as a city.

A Dynasty Begins

Henry's rule over Munich would be short lived. In 1180, he was deposed after refusing to fight for his cousin, Holy Roman Emperor Frederick I, and replaced by Otto von Wittelsbach, starting a royal dynasty that would continue for 738 years. The years that followed were a period of growth and prosperity for the young city, both in size and wealth. Otto II made Munich the ducal residence in 1255 and by the start of the 13th century, it was one of the richest cities in Germany. This rise to stardom was crowned in the early 14th century, when Ludwig IV became Emperor of Germany in 1314 and then Holy Roman Emperor in 1328. Munich was suddenly the centre of power in

Entry of Swedish forces into Munich, in 1632

Germany and Ludwig bestowed it with a salt monopoly, which further enriched the city coffers, and a new wall that defended the burgeoning settlement for the next four centuries.

The Capital of Bavaria

Though Munich would not remain the centre of power beyond Ludwig's reign, the city continued to grow and thrive, becoming the capital of a united Bavaria in 1506. Many of Munich's modern landmarks were built in this period, including the Altes Rathaus (Old City Hall), the Frauenkirche and Peterskirche. Grand building projects continued throughout the 16th century, as Munich was transformed into a centre of the Renaissance and the Counter-Reformation, with lavish new buildings, including Michaelskirche and the Residenz. Munich continued to accrue power and wealth until the double disaster of the 1630s. First, Munich was besieged by Sweden as part of the Thirty Years' War (the Wittelsbachs' decision to quickly surrender and bargain meant it was spared being sacked), then just two years later, the Bubonic Plague killed around a third of the population. The city was shattered, but not defeated, and would soon rebound as it entered the Baroque era, with a new wave of grand buildings projects, most notably the lavish Schloss Nymphenburg.

Duke Henry the Lion and Emperor Frederick Barbarossa

Moments in History

500 BCE
Celts first settle the area around Munich, with a La Tène settlement dating back to 300 BCE found in northern Munich.

5 CE
Bavarian tribes begin to populate the area surrounding modern-day Munich.

550 CE
The Duchy of Bavaria is founded, unifying the various Germanic tribes.

1158
Munich is officially founded by Henry the Lion, as he attempts to control the salt trade in the region.

1506
Upper and Lower Bavaria are united and Munich becomes the official capital.

1810
Crown Prince Ludwig I marries Therese of Saxony-Hildburghausen; the Oktoberfest tradition is created.

1871
Bavaria becomes a federated state of the new German Empire.

1918
Ludwig III flees the city as the state becomes a Republic under Kurt Eisner, ending the rule of the Wittelsbachs.

1939-44
Munich is ravaged by air strikes during the war, with almost three quarters of all buildings damaged.

1972
Munich hosts the Olympic Games, building an underground system and stadium especially for the Games.

1974
West Germany wins the football World Cup in Munich's Olympic Stadium, beating the Netherlands in the final.

2024
Munich opens football's European Championships at the Allianz Arena, hosting five further games during the tournament.

Rise of Modern Munich

The dawn of the 19th century saw Munich invaded again, this time by Napoleon Bonaparte. Yet this occupation was to prove the making of Munich. Napoleon allowed the city's rulers to accrue territory beyond Bavaria and abolished the Holy Roman Empire, paving the way for Bavaria to become an independent state in 1806, with Munich as its capital. The decades that followed saw beautiful Neo-Classical buildings spring up in the expanding districts and the cultural arts flourish. The Alte Pinakothek was built and soon housed a huge collection of paintings; Richard Wagner gave the city fame as a place of music; and the first football club, TSV 1860 München, was founded. This independence ended in 1871, when Bavaria was reluctantly incorporated into Otto von Bismarck's new Germany. The Wittelsbachs retained their status, but lost their power, and by World War I their days were numbered. Munich survived the war unscathed, but its people were starved by Allied blockades and hungry for change. In November 1918, the last Witteslbach, Ludwig III, fled, and the Free State of Bavaria (*Freistaat Bayern*) was proclaimed.

Façade of the Alte Pinakothek around 1900

Modern architecture in the BMW Welt & Museum

Nazi Rule and World War II

In the chaos of post-war Germany, the fledgling Weimar Republic struggled to establish itself, with riots and frequent uprisings. In 1923, Adolf Hitler, accompanied by 3,000 supporters, attempted a coup d'état by marching on Munich's Feldherrnhalle. The putsch failed, but the Weimar Republic remained beset by problems and the Nazis took power in 1933. Munich would be an important Nazi stronghold throughout their rule and the first concentration camp was built at nearby Dachau in 1933. Meaningful resistance was limited to the brave White Rose movement, led by Hans and Sophie Scholl. The onset of World War II was disastrous for Munich: over half the city's building's and around 90 per cent of the Old Town were destroyed in air raids that killed thousands of citizens.

Economic Prosperity

From the ashes of 1945, Munich was carefully reconstructed brick by brick in an effort to preserve its history. Political and financial stability ensured the city quickly rebounded and thanks to the so-called *Wirtschaftswunder* (economic miracle), it was soon thriving again, with a population that passed one million in 1957, and a rapidly developing manufacturing industry. This culminated with the awarding of the 1972 Olympic Games to Munich, an event tragically blighted by a terrorist attack that killed 17 people.

Munich Today

Today, Munich is a cosmopolitan metropolis, able to embrace both its past traditions and its promising future. It retains a thriving cultural scene that continues to evolve through modern spots such as the Museum Brandhorst, a prominent graffiti scene and the ever-popular Oktoberfest. Alongside this, the city has become a hub of technological innovation and startups, often called the "Silicon Valley of Europe", with many multinational companies located in the city. It's this innovative spirit that's helping the city build for the future. Munich was the first German city to create a framework for climate action and aims to be climate-neutral by 2030, demonstrating that this is an ever-evolving city.

TOP 10
EXPERIENCES

Planning the perfect trip to Munich? Whether you're visiting for the first time or making a return trip, there are some things you simply shouldn't miss out on. To make the most of your time – and to enjoy the very best this wonderfully varied city has to offer – be sure to add these experiences to your list.

1 Visit the Museum Quarter
For a taste of Munich's excellent museums, visit the 18 museums and over 40 galleries located in this small area. Start with ancient sculptures at Glyptothek (p95), learn about the Nazi's at the Documentation Centre (p96) and finish with paintings from Rubens to Rembrandt at the Alte Pinakothek (p28).

2 Drink a beer (or two)
Munich loves beer, and the city's many beer halls and gardens are the perfect spots for a Maß (a litre) beer. Join the locals for a lager in the hallowed halls of the 16th-century Hofbräuhaus (p87) or cool down under a chestnut tree with a mug of locally brewed beer in the vast Hirschgarten (p126).

3 Relax in peaceful parks
Glorious green spaces are an integral part of Munich, each an oasis of tranquillity in the busy metropolis. The huge Englischer Garten (p32) is just about every type of park rolled into one (it even has river surfers), while the Botanischer Garten (p127) is perfect for pottering among colourful plants.

4 Attend traditional festivals
Oktoberfest (p42) is the most famous show in town, and for good reason, but there are many other enjoyable events. Welcome spring on a rollercoaster at the fun-filled Frühlingsfest, or enjoy musical, dance and theatre performances at Tollwood (p74) in summer.

5 See a football match

Few things incite the passions of city residents like Bayern Munich. Catch a game at their space-age Allianz Arena ground (p56) or see FC Bayern Women at the Campus ground. Can't get a ticket? Then join locals in a football bar or take a tour of the Allianz Arena.

6 Rove in royal residences

Want to see how Munich's royalty lived? Take a trip to the city's splendid palaces, once home to the Wittelsbach monarchs. Take in the opulent Residenz (p26) in the city centre before heading to the edge of town to see the summer dwelling, Schloss Nymphenburg (p38).

7 Eat a hearty feast

You'll do well to go hungry in Munich. The city specializes in dishes that give that warm, contented feeling, such as hearty dumplings and roasted pork. Get down to Munich's oldest marketplace, Viktualienmarkt (p80), or find a cozy beer hall and tuck in.

8 Explore modern marvels

If you're a fan of modern architecture, Munich has gems aplenty. Contrast the unusual deconstructivist BMW Welt (p126) with the nearby fabric and steel Olympiastadion (p41). Then there's the stacked cubes of Synagogue Ohel Jakob (p80) and an Endless Staircase sculpture.

9 Stroll along the Isar

When Munich's bustling streets feel a little too busy, escape to the serene banks of the Isar, Munich's river. Both riverbanks take you on fascinating trails through the city centre, encompassing peaceful pastures, calming beaches and many a beer garden in which to refuel.

10 Climb every mountain

Head one hour south of Munich for fun in the Alps, including the tallest mountain, Zugspitze (p131). Reach the summit on the 1920s cogwheel train; crisp alpine air and breathtaking views await, as well as some Kaiserschmarrn (a thick, fluffy, shredded pancake).

ITINERARIES

Visiting lavish royal palaces, enjoying a drink in a beer garden, strolling the lanes around Marienplatz: there's a lot to see and do in Munich. With places to eat, drink or take in the view, these itineraries offer ways to spend 2 days and 4 days in Munich.

2 DAYS

Day 1

Morning

Start your two days in Munich with a traditional Bavarian breakfast at Café-Bistro Dallmayr (p91), around the back of Marienplatz (p22), before heading into this beautiful square in the Old Town. Don't rush here, it's worth linger-ing to take in its delights: the onion domes of the medieval Frauenkirche (p24) and both the Old and New Rathaus (p22). If you have a head for heights, take the lift up to the top of the New Rathaus for one of the best views in the city. Come back to earth and wander the narrow lanes around Old Town, spotting Peterskirche (p22), the oldest church in the city, and the resplendent Renais-sance-style Michaelskirche (p82). Just be sure you're back in Marienplatz for 11am to see the famous Glockenspiel

DRINK
Stop for a refreshing cocktail at the elegant Goldene Bar (p106), on the ground floor of the Haus der Kunst, and watch surfers on the adjacent Eisbachwelle.

(p23) in action. After a morning full of exploring, get acquainted with the city's beer culture at the Hofbräuhaus (p87).

Afternoon

After lunch, head east along the boutique-lined Maximilianstraße (p91) to see the seat of the Bavarian state parliament, the Maximilianeum (p109); you may want to pop into a few shops on the way. Take a moment to enjoy a drink at one of the cafés that surround neighbouring Wiener Platz (p112) before moving south, hugging the River Isar, to the Deutsches Museum (p34), one of the largest science museums in the world. Explore its fascinating exhibits, and get hands-on with the interactive elements (a sure fire hit with kids). Round off the day by heading to Blitz (blitz.restaurant), next to the Deutsches Museum, for veg-etarian Mexican food in a riverside beer garden, ideal for watching the sunset.

Day 2

Morning

Fuel up for your day with breakfast at Tambosi (p92), one of Munich's oldest cafés and a great spot for people-

Outdoor seating at a market café on Wiener Platz

watching. Then it's off to spend a few hours at the Residenz palace (p26), one of the city's most iconic buildings and the biggest urban palace in Germany. The building itself shows the changing tastes in architecture and design with Renaissance, Baroque, Rococo and Neo-Classical features all in evidence. Rest a while in the adjacent Hofgarten (p88) before wandering through the underpass to reach the southern tip of the Englischer Garten (p32). If the weather's good, enjoy a sandwich from Fräulein Grüneis (p59) and watch surfers riding waves at the Eisbachwelle (p33). Alternatively, the Café & Restaurant MUSEUM, hidden in the Bayerisches Nationalmuseum (p102), is a lovely choice for a more upmarket lunch, and has a peaceful courtyard to boot.

Visitors exploring exhibits in the Bayerisches Nationalmuseum

Afternoon

Dedicate the afternoon to art and choose your own adventure: fans of more traditional styles should head to the Alte Pinakothek (p28), one of the most important galleries in Europe filled with hundreds of beautiful works from throughout history, while lovers of modern art should go next door, either to the Pinakothek der Moderne (p30) or the Museum Brandhorst (p96). The latter is a more recent addition to Munich's cultural scene, housed in a striking building surrounded by ceramic rods, and features international art from the 1960s onwards. For your final night, enjoy excellent Lebanese cuisine at Baalbek (p99) before sampling the fun bars around the Museum Quarter.

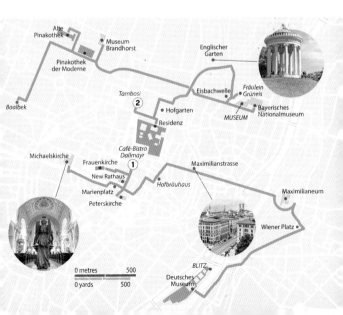

Alte Pinakothek
Museum Brandhorst
Pinakothek der Moderne
Englischer Garten
Baalbek
Tambosi
(2)
Eisbachwelle
Fräulein Grüneis
Hofgarten
Residenz
MUSEUM
Bayerisches Nationalmuseum
Café-Bistro Dallmayr
(1)
Michaelskirche
Frauenkirche
Maximilianstrasse
New Rathaus
Marienplatz
Hofbräuhaus
Maximilianeum
Peterskirche
Wiener Platz
BLITZ
Deutsches Museum

| 0 metres | 500 |
| 0 yards | 500 |

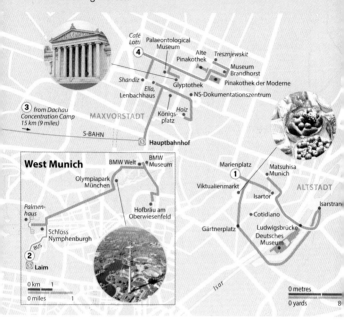

Café Lotti • Palaeontological Museum
④
Alte Pinakothek • Tresznjewskit
Museum Brandhorst
Shandiz • Ella, Lenbachhaus • Glyptothek • Pinakothek der Moderne
NS-Dokumentationszentrum
Hoiz
Königs-platz
③ from Dachau Concentration Camp 15 km (9 miles)
MAXVORSTADT
S-BAHN
Ⓢ Hauptbahnhof

West Munich
BMW Welt • BMW Museum
Olympiapark München
Marienplatz • Matsuhisa Munich
①
Viktualienmarkt
ALTSTADT
Isartor
Isartran
Palmen-haus
Hofbräu am Oberwiesenfeld
Cotidiano
Ⓑ Schloss Nymphenburg
Gärtnerplatz
Ludwigsbrücke Deutsches Museum
② BUS
Ⓢ Laim

Isar

| 0 km | 1 |
| 0 miles | 1 |

| 0 metres | |
| 0 yards | 8 |

4 DAYS

Day 1

Where better to start your four days than by exploring the historic Old Town. After starting in Marienplatz, wander the pretty alleys and streets of the quarter. See if you can visit all three remaining city gates (p82); the Isartor is home to a quirky museum dedicated to Munich's famous comedy couple, Karl Valentin and Liesl Karlstadt. Head south to Viktualienmarkt (p80), the city's oldest marketplace and a great place to try local delicacies and grab a morning coffee. Continue south to Gärtnerplatz, the heart of the historic Glockenbach district with quaint cafés

> 🛍 **SHOP**
> While wandering around the Glochenbachviertel, stop at Man versus Machine (mvsm.coffee), the city's famous third-wave roastery, to enjoy some high-quality coffee.

and independent shops. Pop into a few shops before lunch in Cotidiano (p81). Then hop across the Isar and spend a couple of hours in the Deutsches Museum (p34), before strolling along the river's banks. For dinner, head to Ludwigsbrücke for Japanese food with a Peruvian twist at Matsuhisa (p91).

Day 2

Spend your second morning exploring the extravagant Wittelsbach summer residence, Schloss Nymphenburg (p38). Get there via the S-Bahn to Laim and then the 51 or 151 bus. The palace is magnificent to tour, but don't miss the gardens, which are always beautifully manicured and the perfect place for a leisurely stroll. In summer visitors can also ride a gondola in the central canal. Grab lunch at the palace itself, in the stylish Palmenhaus, which has excellent outdoor seating on which to soak up the sun. Suitably refuelled, walk (or take a tram) to the Olympiapark (*p40*), where you can spend the afternoon wandering around the huge park and visiting the stadiums built for the 1972 Olympics. Motor heads (and architecture fans) will enjoy the exhibits in the BMW Museum and BMW Welt (*p126*) at the northern edge of the park. Finish with traditional fare and a local beer at Hofbräu am Oberwiesenfeld (*oberwiesenfeld.de*).

Day 3

Escape the confines of the city for the morning and take the train to the Dachau Concentration Camp (*p134*), the Nazi's first concentration camp in Germany. It might not be the easiest visit, but a tour of the site is important to understand its history. Return to Munich to grab a bite to eat at Ella, the airy café in the Lenbachhaus gallery (*p95*). Continue the historical theme of today at the NS-Dokumentationszentrum (*p96*), a museum on the Nazi period, before strolling over to the Palace of Justice (*p98*) to see the exhibit dedicated to the White Rose resistance group. Finish off the day with dinner at upmarket Hoiz (*p99*).

EAT
Want to try the best hand made ice cream in the city? Then find your way to True & 12 ice cream parlour (*trueand12.com*), close to the Deutsches Museum, where delicious sustainable ice cream is made.

Day 4

After a hearty breakfast at Café Lotti (*p99*), enjoy one last day of culture, starting at Königsplatz (*p95*). Either visit the Glyptothek (*p95*) sculptures museum or visit one of the Pinakothek galleries: the Alte (*p28*) is great for classic art while the Moderne (*p30*) will appeal to lovers of contemporary pieces. Stop off at Shandiz (*shandiz.de*) for excellent Persian food, and then continue on to to the Museum Brandhorst (*p96*) for eclectic modern art (Warhol, Koons and Hirst are on display, among others), or take a trip to the Palaeontology Museum (*p98*), home to several skeletons of ancient beasts. Your final stop is for a hearty dinner and drinks at Tresznjewski (*p99*), the perfect place to round off an exciting trip to Munich.

Fountain in the Baroque garden of the Nymphenburg Palace

TOP 10 HIGHLIGHTS

Neuschwanstein castle in winter

EXPLORE THE
HIGHLIGHTS

There are some sights in Munich you simply shouldn't miss, and it's these attractions that make the Top 10. Discover what makes each one a must-see on the following pages.

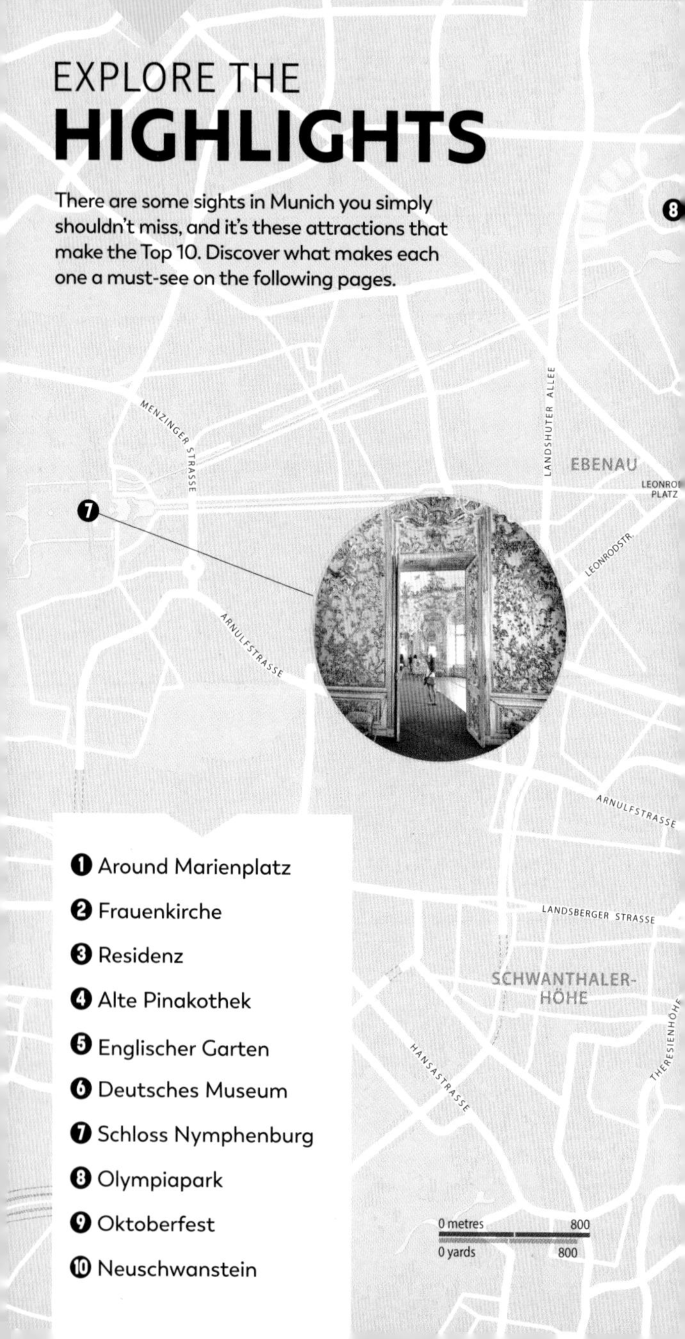

❶ Around Marienplatz

❷ Frauenkirche

❸ Residenz

❹ Alte Pinakothek

❺ Englischer Garten

❻ Deutsches Museum

❼ Schloss Nymphenburg

❽ Olympiapark

❾ Oktoberfest

❿ Neuschwanstein

| 0 metres | 800 |
| 0 yards | 800 |

Around Munich

Munich

Landsberg am Lech · A96 · Grünwald

Ammersee · Starnberg · Schäftlarn

B17 · B2 · Starnberger See

Wessobrunn · B472

Peißenberg · Seeshaupt · Geretsried

Steingaden · Penzberg · Bad Tölz

Rottenbuch · B472

Ettal · A95 · Kochel am See

0 km   20
0 miles   20

10

Olympiasee

ACKERMANNSTRASSE

SCHWABING

Kleinhesseloher See

ELISABETHSTRASSE

NORDENDSTR.

FRANZ-JOSEPH-STR.

DACHAUER STRASSE

SCHLEISSHEIMER STR.

THERESIENSTRASSE

ARCISSTRASSE

NYMPHENBURGER STR.

GABELSBERGERSTRASSE

4

5

KÖNIGS-PLATZ

MARSSTRASSE

MAX-VORSTADT

PRINZREGENTENSTRASSE

Isar

ELISENSTR.

MAXIMILIANS-PLATZ

ODEONS-PLATZ

3

BAYERSTRASSE

NEUHAUSER STR.

2

MAXIMILIANSTRASSE

LEHEL

HERZOG-HEINRICH-STR.

SONNENSTR.

1

ALTSTADT

9

LUDWIGS-VORSTADT

TAL

FRAUEN-STR.

BAVARIARING

ERHARDTSTRASSE

6

AU

AROUND MARIENPLATZ

🚇 N3–4

Marienplatz has been the heart of Munich for centuries and is known as the starting point for exploring the capital. The square is studded with historic structures, one of them being the Glockenspiel clock tower, which attracts tourists and locals alike for its performing mechanical figures. Today, it's also known for its famous Christkindlmarkt (Christmas Fair).

1 Altes Rathaus

The old town hall (p79) dates back to 1470 and is situated in the eastern corner of Marienplatz. Gothic in style, it features both a grand hall and a tower (formerly the gateway to the city). Inside is the Spielzeugmuseum (toy museum), which displays a selection of antique toys.

2 Odeonsplatz

A wander around Odeonsplatz shows why Munich is sometimes called "Italy's northernmost city". This square is bordered by the Italianate, late Baroque Theatinerkirche (p88), the Residenz, and the Hofgarten and its archways. On the Old Town side, the square is bounded by the Feldherrnhalle, which honours the heroes of the Bavarian army. It was built in 1844 by Friedrich von Gärtner, who drew inspiration from the Florentine Loggia dei Lanzi.

3 Dallmayr

Behind the town hall once stood the green oasis of Marienhof. It has now become the site of an S-Bahn station. The impressive yellow-and-white façade on the right belongs to the well-known foodie paradise of Dallmayr (p91).

4 Peterskirche

Munich's oldest parish church (p79), Peterskirche sits atop the highest point in the old town. Its Renaissance tower, known as "Alter Peter" (Old Peter), is one of the city's best-known landmarks featuring eight clocks, seven bells

and a viewing gallery, which has a splendid view over the Old Town.

5 Residenz

Max-Joseph-Platz is the site of the 130-room Residenz (p88), a palace that functioned as a home to Bavarian monarchs for five centuries. The buildings date back to 1385, when the Neuveste (new fortress) was built in the part of Munich enclosed by city walls. Its monumental façades and courtyards are open to the public, and the Residenz-museum is housed inside.

6 Sendlinger Straße

This shopping district (p83) has two main

Statue of the Count von Tilly on the Odeonsplatz

attractions: the late Baroque Asamkirche and, right next door, the Asam-Haus *(p81)* with its impressive façade.

7 Pedestrian Zone
Munich's most popular traffic-free zone starts just to the west of Marienplatz and extends through to Karlsplatz. This is a hub of shopping and also the location of the late Renaissance Michaelskirche *(p82)*.

8 Nationaltheater
Modelled on a Greek temple, the Nationaltheater *(p87)* is one of the largest opera stages in the world. This structure has seen the premieres of many significant operas over the years and has been destroyed and rebuilt twice in its lifetime.

The 19th-century Neues Rathaus at Marienplatz

Cheese stall, Viktualienmarkt

TOP TIP

The Glochenspiel chimes at 11am and noon daily, and also at 5pm in summer.

9 Viktualienmarkt
Originated in 1807 and featuring some 140 stalls, this daily food market *(p80)* is the city's oldest and most picturesque. The southernmost end is home to the beer cellar and restaurant, Der Pschorr, and the grain market, Schrannenhalle, which offer a wide variety of Italian delicacies.

10 Neues Rathaus
This Neo-Gothic town hall *(p78)* was built between 1867 and 1909. At the top of the tower sits the city mascot, the Münchner Kindl (Munich Child). It is also home to the famous Glockenspiel. Each day, the bells ring out a carillon while mechanical knights enact a joust and perform the Dance of the Coopers.

FRAUENKIRCHE

📍 M3 🏛 Frauenplatz 🕐 8am–8pm Mon–Sat 🌐 muenchner-dom.de 📷 🖼

The Frauenkirche is the largest Gothic hall church in southern Germany. It was built between 1468–88 by Jörg von Halspach and Lucas Rottaler to replace an earlier Romanesque church; the 20-year construction time was a record for the period. The domes atop its two almost 100-m (328-ft) towers dominate the city's skyline – no buildings are permitted to be built higher.

1 The Devil's Footprint
Legend tells that the dip in the floor at the entrance to the church is from the Devil's footprint. When the Devil lost a bet with Jörg von Halspach, he was so furious that he stamped his foot, leaving an imprint forever here.

📷 VIEW
Climb up the south tower's narrow spiral staircase before entering a lift to enjoy the panoramic views from the roof. This is one of the best vantage points in the city.

2 Bridal Doorway
The southeastern entrance is adorned with delicate figurines and other elaborate embellishments.

3 The Emperor's Tomb
The intricately carved tomb of Emperor Ludwig IV of Bavaria was completed in 1622 by Hans Krumpper. A Mannerist canopy of black marble covers the tomb, and the sarcophagus is surrounded by the figures of four kneeling knights.

4 Choir Carvings
The choir stalls and screens in the chancel display figures and reliefs added between 1495 and 1502 by Erasmus Grasser.

5 Vaulted Ceilings
The original vaulted ceiling, with its star pattern, was destroyed during the bombings of World War II, and meticulously restored in 1990–93.

6 Organ
The main organ is one of four in the cathedral and was built by Georg Jann in 1994. It is a gigantic instrument, with tubes ranging in size from drainpipes to straws.

The Frauenkirche, against the city skyline

8 Cathedral Windows

The windows were added at various times over the centuries. Some of the original Gothic and stained-glass windows are still in situ. Viewed from the portal, a double row of 22 pillars runs down the nave, hiding the windows and giving the appearance of a wall.

7 Memminger Altar

From the chancel to the right and left of the Mariensäule (column), it is possible to see parts of the winged Memminger Altar, designed in around 1500 by Claus Strigel. It incorporates stunning reliefs by Ignaz Günther and a superb Rococo Madonna.

9 Statue of St Christopher

This larger than life-size figure, carved in around 1525, is an example of the dramatic style of the late Gothic period.

10 Towers
🕐 10am–5pm Mon–Sat, 11:30am–5pm Sun 🔇

The two towers, with their Renaissance

FRAUENKIRCHE'S BELLS

The church houses one of Germany's most important bell collections - five from the Middle Ages and two from the Baroque period. The biggest, nicknamed Susanna, weighs almost 7 tonnes (8 tons) and has a diameter of around 2 m (7 ft). It was built in 1490 and is one of the biggest church bells in Bavaria.

domes, were modelled on the Dome of the Rock in Jerusalem. Only the South Tower, which features a small shop, can be climbed by visitors. Entry is free for kids under 7 years.

Clockwise from below
The nave with its tall pillars; the church's grand main organ; stunning stained-glass window

RESIDENZ

N3 ⬜ Residenzstraße 1 ⬜ Apr–mid-Oct: 9am–6pm daily; mid-Oct–Mar: 10am–5pm daily ⬜ residenz-muenchen.de

Located in the heart of the city, this former residence of Bavarian kings began in 1385 as a moated castle and eventually grew into an extensive complex with ten courtyards. The largest urban castle in the country, it has over 150 rooms open to the public and exhibits a fusion of styles, from the Baroque Cuvilliés-Theater to the Mannerist Reiche Kapelle.

1 Grüne Galerie
The Reiches Zimmer suite, designed by François Cuvilliés the Elder, is home to the Green Gallery, in which Elector Karl Albrecht hosted a great many parties.

2 Hofgarten
Shaded by linden trees on the north side of the Residenz, this Renaissance garden,

Superb ceiling frescoes in the Antiquarium

dating back to 1613, exudes a southern European air. The Temple of Diana, designed by Heinrich Schön the Elder, stands at the heart of the garden's network of pathways.

3 Antiquarium
Commissioned by Duke Albrecht V, this 69-m- (226-ft-) long vault is embellished with stunning allegorical frescoes, grotesque paintings and Bavarian landscapes.

120 m (130 yd)

Residenz Site Plan

4 Hofkapelle
This stuccoed, two-storey chapel was built in 1601–14 by Hans Krumpper. Courtiers

TOP TIP

Not all of the rooms in the Residenz are wheelchair accessible.

The Brunnenhof, one of the inner courtyards

would congregate down below, while the ruling family would attend Mass from the upper galleries.

5 Lions

The front of the Residenz building is guarded by four bronze lions bearing shields. All of their muzzles are worn down, which is due to the local tradition of stroking them for good luck when passing by.

6 Inner Courtyards

Of the various courtyards, look out for the

Grottenhof and the octagonal-shaped Brunnenhof. The largest is the Apothekenhof, while the smallest is the one by the Cuvilliés-Theater.

7 Cuvilliés-Theater

◻ Mid-Mar–mid-Oct: 9am–6pm daily; mid-Oct–Mar: 10am–5pm daily ⚡

This theatre, built by François Cuvilliés the Elder in 1751–5, is considered the most beautiful Rococo theatre in Europe. It once staged magnificent Baroque operas and is still used today for performances of all kinds.

8 Reiche Kapelle

With its ebony altar, coloured marble and gilded reliefs, Maximilian I's elaborate private chapel (1607) is a prime example of Mannerist architecture.

9 Staatliche Münzsammlung

◻ 10am–5pm Tue–Sun
ⓦ staatliche-muenz sammlung.de ⚡

This museum is home to the world's largest collection of coins. It also has banknotes, medals and cut stones, including antique gems, on display.

10 Schatzkammer

The 16th-century treasury contains the Wittelsbach dynasty's crown jewels, gold reliquaries, porcelain and other treasures.

Figurine at the Schatzkammer

ALTE PINAKOTHEK

F4 🄰 Barer Straße 🄾 10am–8pm Tue & Wed, 10am–6pm Thu–Sun
🄦 pinakothek.de 🄵🄶

One of Munich's top-class art galleries, the Alte Pinakothek is a treasure trove of European painting. Its extensive collection includes more than 700 artworks from the 14th to 18th centuries, with pieces by artistic masters including Rembrandt, Rubens, Botticelli and Brueghel. Exploring the Neo-Classical hallways of this elegant gallery is a must for any art-lover.

1 El Greco's Disrobing of Christ

The dramatic *Disrobing of Christ* by El Greco, created in 1580–95, is one of three versions of this famous work. It forms part of an exceptional collection of Spanish paintings.

2 The Portrait of Karl V

This portrait of Emperor Karl V was once attributed to the Italian artist Titian, but was in fact painted by Lambert Sustris, a Dutch painter who worked in his studio.

3 Rembrandt's Descent from the Cross

The rich collection of 17th-century Dutch art includes an outstanding series of Baroque Passion scenes by Rembrandt. The dramatic lighting in *Descent from the Cross* characterizes the artist's 1633 masterpiece, which was a stark contrast to the idealized representations of Christ typical of the time. The figure in blue is a self-portrait.

4 Dürer's Four Apostles

The gallery's Dürer collection documents his development from *Self-Portrait in Fur Coat* (1500) to the *Four Apostles* (1526), painted two years before his death.

Clockwise from right
Hals' portrait of Willem van Heythuysen; Brueghel's *Land of Cockaigne;* **Dürer's** *Four Apostles;* **the stately façade of the museum**

Admiring artworks by Rubens

5 Rubens' The Rape of the Daughters of Leucippus

In this high Baroque masterpiece dating from 1618, Rubens depicts a mythical tangle of human and horse. It can be found in the Flemish collection, which comprises one of the largest collection of works by the artist.

6 Hals' Willem van Heythuysen

Frans Hals' painting of the Haarlem cloth merchant is an outstanding example of Dutch portraiture.

7 Altdorfer's Battle of Alexander at Issus

Albrecht Altdorfer of Regensburg, a painter of the Danube School, is represented by his 1529 painting *Battle of Issus*, which depicts the decisive moment of Alexander the Great's victory over the Persian King Darius.

8 Holbein's Presentation of Jesus at the Temple

This late Gothic piece (1502) by Hans Holbein the Elder forms part of the Kaisheim altar.

9 Botticelli's Lamentation of Christ

Italian master painter Sandro Botticelli's painting from around 1490 is renowned for its red tones, stark contrasts, strong effects of light and shadow, and curved lines. It is generally considered one of the great masterpieces of Italian Renaissance painting.

MUSEUM GUIDE

The Alte Pinakothek's collections are spread across two floors. The ground floor holds Flemish paintings from the 16th and 17th centuries. On the first floor are works by German painters as well as Spanish Netherlandish, Italian Flemish, French and Dutch paintings. Some of the masterpieces from Neue Pinakothek (closed for renovation until 2029) are temporarily housed on the ground floor.

10 Brueghel's Land of Cockaigne

Pieter Brueghel the Elder, the most significant artist of the Flemish School, offers a satirical depiction of gluttony and idleness in this painting from 1567, which is based on a tale by Hans Sachs.

Pinakothek der Moderne

Wide range of exhibits at the Design Museum

1. The Classic Modern Collection
This collection comprises artworks from the early 20th century up to 1960 and has works by Modersohn-Becker, Kirchner, Nolde, Braque, Picasso, Klee and Beckmann, among others.

2. Surrealism
The Surrealist pieces in the museum come from the Wormland Collection. Among the highlights are Salvador Dalí's *The Enigma of Desire* (1929) and Max Ernst's *Fireside Angel* (1937).

3. The Contemporary Art Collection
This section documents the art scene from 1960 onwards and includes works by de Kooning, Bacon, Beuys, Baselitz, Polke, Warhol, Flavin, Wall and Twombly.

4. The Design Museum
Modern utilitarian objects are the theme of this 80,000-strong collection at Die Neue Sammlung – The Design Museum. The exhibits here range from Thonet chairs and Pop furniture right through to objects from the world of aerodynamics and digital culture. It also displays Dutch designer Hella Jongerius's *Bowl with Hippopotamus*, along with works by German ceramicist Beate Kuhn.

5. Installations
Permanent installations at the museum include Joseph Beuys' *The End of the Twentieth Century* (1983) and works from Dan Flavin's *"monuments" for V. Tatlin* (1964).

6. The Graphic Arts Collection
This collection comprises tens of thousands of drawings and prints, though only a fraction is ever on display at any one time. Highlights include works by Old Masters such as Rembrandt and Michelangelo, in addition to pieces by Cézanne, Baselitz and Wols.

7. Drawings
Among the highlights of this collection are Raphael's red chalk drawing of *Mercury and Psyche* (1517/18) and Franz Marc's *The Tower of Blue Horses* (1912) in ink.

8. The Architecture Collection
Some 350,000 drawings and plans, 100,000 photographs and 500 models are presented in rotating exhibits on the ground floor.

9. Drawings and Sketches
With a focus on German architecture from the 18th to the 21st centuries, these exhibits include drawings and sketches by Balthasar Neumann, Leo von Klenze and Le Corbusier.

10. Design Vision
This two-storey display cabinet showcases objects that illuminate the full spectrum of the gallery's collection, ranging from visionary ideas through to everyday objects.

A BUILDING OF RUBBLE

Remains of the Alte Pinakothek after it was destroyed by World War II bombings in 1945

The Alte Pinakothek might be one of the oldest galleries in the world, but the building is actually deceptively new. Early in World War II, the Alte Pinakothek's collection was relocated as a safeguard – a prophetic move as more than a third of the building would be entirely destroyed by bombing and the rest burned out. After the war, the Bavarian architect Hans Döllgast petitioned for a "creative reconstruction", where the surviving skeleton of the building would be kept, but missing parts would be filled by using rubble from air raids. It was a way of keeping the city's cultural heritage alive while remembering the horrors of the war. Döllgast had the idea in 1946, but it took six years of campaigning to have his plans approved by the state, as other architects argued that a complete demolition would be a better option. When walking around the Alte Pinakothek today, it's possible to see Döllgast's reconstructive work among the older parts of the structure; the imperfect building a reminder of the terrors of the time.

Façade of the Alte Pinakothek showing its reconstructed parts

ENGLISCHER GARTEN

📍 H1–G4

One of the largest inner-city parks in Europe, the Englischer Garten was born from the marshy banks of the Isar as a park for the use of the army. Later opened to the public in 1792, it remains popular among locals and visitors alike, who come to walk or jog its meandering paths, enjoy a bite to eat or simply relax.

1 Rumford Monument

This monument depicts the American officer Sir Benjamin Thompson, later known as Count von Rumford, who ordered the creation of the park.

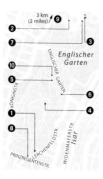

2 Kleinhesseloher See

This lake can be found in the northernmost corner of the park. It is the perfect spot to take a rowing boat or pedalo onto the water. The shores of the lake are home to a scenic beer garden.

3 Seehaus

📍 G2 🏠 Kleinhesseloher 3

The beer garden belonging to the Seehaus restaurant occupies an idyllic spot on Kleinhesseloher See, partly shaded by the nearby trees. If the weather is good, it stays open out of season.

4 Monopteros

This Neo-Classical round temple was built in 1836 by Leo von Klenze. It sits atop an artificial hill, which is a popular spot all year round, attracting sunbathers in the summer and tobogganists in winter. The Monopteros also offers panoramic views of the city.

EAT
The Englischer Garten has four restaurants with attached beer gardens. The largest one is at the Chinesischer Turm.

Neo-Classical Monopteros temple

of Munich's best beer gardens, which is open from May to September.

6 Orangerie
📍 G3 🏛 Englischer Garten 1A

The former orangery now serves as a space to showcase artworks by local artists. It is open to public for exhibitions only.

5 Chinesischer Turm
📍 G3 🏛 Englischer Garten 3

The Chinese Tower (p68) is one of the city's most emblematic landmarks. Standing five storeys high, the wooden pagoda in the traditional Chinese style dates back to 1789 and has burned down and been rebuilt several times. It has a restaurant that is open all year round. At the foot of the tower is one

7 Friedrich-Ludwig-von-Sckell Monument

This memorial, designed by Leo von Klenze in 1824, was built in memory of the park's designer.

TOP TIP

Rent a bike (mucbike. de) from the main entrance to explore the garden trails.

Surfing on the Eisbach river

8 Surfers on the Eisbach

Undeterred by the icy waters, surfers engage with the Eisbach rapids at the southernmost tip of the park.

9 Sheep Herd

In the northern part of the garden, visitors will encounter a herd of sheep grazing in the grassy fields. This part of the garden is more rugged and densely wooded compared to the carefully manicured lawns that can be seen further south.

10 Historisches Karussell
📍 G3 🏛 Englischer Garten 4 🕐 Apr–Oct: from 2pm daily (from 1pm in summer hols)

Right next to the Chinesischer Turm is a Biedermeier-style children's roundabout, complete with carriages, sleighs and whimsical wooden animals. Open since 1913, it is still in use today.

Busy beer garden at Chinesischer Turm

DEUTSCHES MUSEUM

📍 F5 🏛 Museumsinsel 1 🕐 9am–5pm daily 🚫 1 Jan, Shrove Tue, Good Fri, 1 May, 1 Nov, 24, 25 & 31 Dec 🌐 deutsches-museum.de 📷📱

The world's largest museum of technology and engineering was founded in 1903 by German engineer Oskar von Miller. It is located in a building on Museumsinsel and currently houses around 25,000 exhibits. There are two other branches; the Verkehrszentrum near the Theresienwiese and the Flugwerft Schleißheim, north of the centre.

1 Enigma Machine

The Enigma encoding machine built during World War II is a fine example of early information technology. The Image Script Codes collection has three machines on display: one naval and two from the army.

2 Photography and Film

Movie buffs can learn about the history of film from Daguerre to DVD, and how filmmaking has developed over the years at this fascinating exhibit.

3 Health

A gigantic body fills the room in this exhibit devoted to understanding the human body – walk into a head or a rib cage, discover how your heart functions and explore a reconstructed 18th-century pharmacy.

Key to Floorplan
- Level LG
- Level 0
- Level 1
- Level 2
- Levels 3–6

Deutsches Museum Floorplan

4 Kids' Kingdom

Young children (3–8 years) can learn about science and technology in fun, imaginative ways in this sprawling play area. Exhibits include a giant guitar, a creative marble run and a hall of mirrors.

5 Physics and Atomic Science

The physics and atomic science sections are a great introduction to all things science, with interactive exhibitions and model recreations of famous experiments, including a re-creation of Schrödinger's cat and Foucault's pendulum.

Display in the food exhibition

6 Modern Aviation

Tracing the history of aviation since 1945, this exhibition shows the evolution of flight in recent decades. There's a flight simulator and information on air-traffic control and flight safety.

7 Agriculture and Food

Learn where food comes from and how it's made. This exhibition illustrates the development of farming equipment from the simplest tools to types of ploughs and modern farm machinery. It has a model brewery and a prototype of a field robot.

8 Robotics

The robotics exhibition room features robots designed for household tasks, play and medicine. Designed like a virtual

Browsing exhibits in the Modern Aviation section

space, the room features several early prototypes of "human" robots, a guitar-playing robot and high-tech machines of the (near) future.

9 Musical Instruments

Over 2,000 musical instruments are on display in chronological order here. Across three rooms, visitors can trace the important stages in the history of musical instruments from the Renaissance right up to the present day. Exhibits include a historic 16th-century harpsichord, the Ahrend organ and the Moog IIIP synthesiser, the first such instrument in Germany.

10 Other Branches

The Deutsches Museum has two other branches in addition to the main site. The Flugwerft Schleißheim focuses on the history of aviation and displays over 50 historic aircraft in an old aeroplane hanger. The Verkehrszentrum is the largest transport museum in the world, with historic trains, cars, carriages and bicycles.

An exhibit in the Robotics room

TOP TIP

Download the official app to explore the museum on a virtual tour.

Flugwerft Schleißheim and Verkehrszentrum Highlights

1. Alois Wolfmüller's Glider
Dating back to 1907, this glider, built in Landsberg am Lech, is the oldest original aircraft displayed in the Flugwerft Schleißheim and still in the condition it flew in. Wolfmüller donated the glider to the museum in 1934, however the tail was missing and wasn't found until 1991. Incredibly, it only weighs 38 kg (84 lb).

2. The Glass Workshop
Visitors can enter a viewing gallery in the Flugwerft's hangar and watch the staff at work to see how the museum's aircraft are repaired and restored.

3. VJ 101 C-X2
At the height of the Cold War in the 1960s, several leading German aviation companies combined to produce this experimental fighter. It never went into production, but the prototype was used throughout the 1960s and 1970s for experimental test flight. What makes it even more unique is that it was the first plane to take-off vertically and was the first German plane to reach super-sonic speed at 1,320 km/h (820 mph) at an altitude of 6,000 m (19,700 ft).

4. Lilienthal's Glider
One of the oldest aircraft in the Flugwerft Schleißheim's collection is the original strap-on wings that Otto Lilienthal used to attempt manned flight. Lilienthal was one of the pioneers of aviation and flew 80 m (260 ft) from an artificial hill in Berlin. Sadly, the original wings are being restored by the museum and are no longer on display. Instead, a life-sized replica is on display alongside other early aircraft, allowing visitors to marvel at the wing-span and the undoubted bravery of this German aviation pioneer.

5. Müller DDHM 22
It may look like an antique, but Herbert Müller's tiny, self-constructed biplane actually dates from 1999. It took Müller 22 years to build and has a wingspan of just 5.2 m (17 ft). The DDHM 22 made a maiden voyage on 23 September 2000, but this was also its last flight: Müller's wife forbid him from flying it again, considering it unsafe.

6. Ford Model T
In the Verkehrszentrum's main hall is this 1922 example of Ford's incredibly

Planes on display at the Flugwerft Schleißheim

popular Model T. This version has a four-cylinder four-stroke engine and could reach a maximum speed of 70 km/h (45 mph)

7. S 3/6

This beautiful steam engine from 1912 is on display in the Verkehrszentrum's second hall. With a top speed of 120 km/h (75 mph), the train was at the cutting-edge of technology and in service for over 40 years. By the time it was decom-missioned, the train had travelled a total of 2.5 million km (1.5 million miles). Be sure to check the museum's schedule as the train's engine is brought to life several times a day.

8. Puffing Billy

Visit hall three of the Verkehrszentrum to see a replica of the world's first oper-ational steam locomotive, known as "Puffing Billy." Built by William Hedley in England in 1814, the original ran on iron rails and was used to haul coal wagons from a mine close to Wylam, in the north of England. The replica itself is still historic, dating from 1906, and the museum still fires up the engine each day.

The Ford Model T at the Verkehrszentrum

9. Benz-Patent-Motorwagen

Invented by the German engineer Carl Benz, this 1885 "Benz patent motorcar" is the first machine to be considered a car, despite only having three-wheels. It's one-cylinder engine may have only produced a top speed of 12 km/h (7 mph), but it still completed a 180 km (110 miles) journey piloted by Benz's wife, Bertha.

10. Model Railway

This railway layout, with a scale of 1:87, in the Verkehrszentrum's third hall delights adults and kids. It depicts a typical German town with small stations, roads with tram and bus stops, a cog-wheel railway and even a harbour. Time your visit to watch the model in action. Shows are at 1:30pm every day.

S 3/6 engine at the Verkehrszentrum

SCHLOSS NYMPHENBURG

📍 A2–3 & B2–3 🌐 schloss-nymphenburg.de 🚉🚋

To celebrate the birth of their son Max Emanuel in 1662, Duke Ferdinand Maria gifted his wife Henriette Adelaide of Savoy an Italianate-style summer palace to the west of Munich. Over the course of 300 years, the original ornamental garden was expanded into a vast park comprising Baroque gardens, a system of canals, and small pavilions dotted throughout the grounds.

1 The Palace
📍 B3 🕐 Apr–mid-Oct: 9am–6pm daily; mid-Oct–Mar: 10am–4pm daily 🚉

Elector Max Emanuel and Karl Albrecht expanded the original villa by adding buildings designed by Enrico Zuccalli and Joseph Effner. Arcaded galleries connect them to the main building.

2 Lackkabinett
This room was designed in 1764 by Cuvilliés the Elder. Chinese black laquer motifs on wood panelling are reprised in the Rococo ceiling fresco.

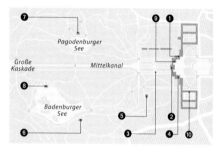

3 Palace Gardens
📍 A3 🕐 6am–6pm daily (Apr & Oct: to 8pm; May–Sep: to 9:30pm)

Symmetrically designed French gardens to the rear of the palace give way to an English-style landscaped park, which was created by using the existing forest. The gardens are home to a number of individual pavilions.

4 Gallery of Beauties
Ludwig I commissioned court artist Joseph Stieler to create these portraits of noblewomen, townswomen and dancers, including Lola Montez, the Irish mistress of King Ludwig I.

5 Amalienburg
📍 A3 🕐 Apr–mid-Oct: 9am–6pm daily 🚉

Built by François Cuvilliés the Elder between 1734 and 1739 for the Electress Amalia, this small hunting lodge is

Façade of the Schloss Nymphenburg

Opulent interior of the Steinerner Saal

a masterpiece of European Rococo. Its richly decorated circular hall, or Hall of Mirrors, was covered with fine shellwork. The windows, doors and mirrors create the illusion of an open pavilion.

6 Badenburg

Featuring a ballroom and two-bathing halls complete with a heated pool, this pavilion is definitely worth a visit. Three of the rooms are lined with Chinese-style wallpaper.

7 Pagodenburg

This elegant 18th-century pavilion with an octagonal floorplan combines Western and Eastern ornamentation to stunning effect.

8 Monopteros

Between 1804 and 1823, Friedrich L von Sckell created a landscaped park behind the palace. During this time, Monopteros, the Apollo temple, was built on the Badenburger See.

Ludwig II's coach, Marstall-museum

9 Steinerner Saal

Upon entering the palace, visitors walk into a spacious ballroom. The windows on either side are embellished in a Rococo style by Johann B Zimmermann and Cuvilliés the Elder in the reign of Max III Joseph.

10 Marstall-museum

This building houses over 40 coaches, carriages and sleighs that once belonged to the Bavarian rulers. Highlights include the French-Rococo coronation coach of Emperor Karl VII, the gilded state coach of Ludwig II and portraits of Karl's favourite horses.

OLYMPIAPARK

📍 D1 🏠 Spiridon-Louis-Ring 21 🌐 olympiapark.de

In preparation for the 1972 Olympic Games, a former airfield and parade ground were transformed into an Olympic park, featuring hills, an artificial lake, a communications tower and sports facilities across an area measuring 3 sq km (1 sq mile). The elegant and airy Olympic stadium, complete with a transparent, curved, tensile roof, is still considered to be a masterpiece of modern architecture.

1 Olympic Skating Rink

The skating rink is the perfect place to bring the kids on winter days. In the evening there's disco skating. Ice skates are available for hire.

2 Olympic Hall

This venue holds up to 15,500 spectators beneath a section of tensile roof, which is suspended from 58 pylons. In addition to sporting events, the hall also hosts concerts and trade fairs.

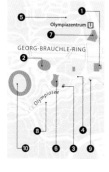

Celebrity hand prints on the Walk Of Stars

3 Kino am Olympiasee

Enjoy a summer evening at the open-air cinema by the lake, with films often shown in their original language.

4 Walk of Stars

Since 2003, a walkway by the Olympic lake has celebrated pop culture icons with concrete star slabs. Those immortalized here include Iron Maiden, Kylie Minogue and Rod Stewart.

5 Olympic Village

Originally built to house athletes during the games,

this complex is now home to around 60,000 people. It's worth a stroll through the student housing area, which has many colourful buildings and a warm community feel.

6 Olympia-Schwimmhalle

🕐 Hours vary, check website 🌐 swm.de
One of the largest in Europe, this aquatic centre has five pools, a 10-m (33-ft) diving board, saunas, a jacuzzi, sunbathing areas, a gym and wellness features.

7 BMW Welt
BMW's car delivery and exhibition centre

TOP TIP

Hop on the on-site railway for a tour through the history of the Olympic park.

Cars in the BMW Welt showroom

(p126) is the epitome of dynamism and elegance. This ultra-modern showroom hosts a variety of events and also contains shops, a café, and one of the best restaurants in Munich, the two Michelin-starred EssZimmer (p126).

8 Lake and Park
Much of this site is purpose-built, including the artificial lake, fed by the Nymphenburg Canal – boats can be hired in summer – and the hills, which were created by covering piles of war debris with turf.

9 Sea Life
This aquarium (p61) is home to an array of underwater creatures, including seahorses, rays and tropical fish. The shark tunnel is a highlight.

10 Olympia-stadion

🕐 10am–8pm daily 🔗
With a capacity of 69,250 spectators, the massive Olympic stadium is now used to host concerts and events.

The superbly landscaped Olympiapark

OKTOBERFEST

📍 J4–5 & K4–5 🏠 Theresienwiese 🕐 Mid-Sep–early Oct 🌐 oktoberfest.de

With around 7 million visitors consuming 7 million litres (12 million pints) of beer, Munich's Oktoberfest is the largest beer festival in the world. The grounds of Theresienwiese are transformed with colourful beer tents run by the city's top six traditional breweries, alongside fair rides and food vendors selling gingerbread hearts and fresh pretzels.

1 O'Zapft Is!
The festival officially begins at noon on the first Saturday of Oktoberfest. During the opening ceremony, Munich's mayor taps the first beer barrel in the Schottenhamel tent and declares to the crowds "O'zapft is!" (It's tapped!), as the beer starts to flow.

2 Arrival of the Wiesn-Wirte
The arrival of the landlords (on Saturday) is the prelude to the opening of the Wiesn. Their carriages are drawn by brightly decorated horses from the brewery.

3 Hearts
Every year, old and new messages appear on these traditional gingerbread hearts on sale at the festival. They make perfect souvenirs.

> **TOP TIP**
>
> Oktoberfest has its own police station, health centre, a lost child point and an ATM.

4 Bavaria Statue
In 1843, Ludwig I commissioned Leo von Klenze to build the

Shopping for gingerbread hearts

Enjoying drinks in a
festive beer tent

 DRINK
Although the
main drink is beer,
you'll also find other
concoctions, such as
beer mixed with
wines, lemonade
(Radlers), ciders
(Apfelsaftschorle)
and liquors.

spectators at the festival
every year since 1948.

Rohmeshalle (Hall of
Fame) on the Theresien-
höhe, which houses
the busts of famous
Bavarians. The colos-
sal statue embodying
Bavaria rises up in
front. A platform inside
its head offers a spec-
tacular view of the
festival area.

5 Memorial
On 26 September
1980, a bomb exploded
at the festival, tragic-
ally killing 13 people
and injuring over 200
more. A memorial stone
by Friedrich Koller stands
here as a reminder of
this neo-Nazi attack.

6 Beer Tents
⏰ 10am–11:30pm
Mon–Fri (from 9am
Sat & Sun); Käfer's
Wiesenschänke:
10am–1am daily
In the large beer tents,
such as the Pschorr-
Bräurosl, alcohol is
king. Patrons link arms
and sway to the music

of brass bands, and
challenge each other
to drink another Maß
(litre) of beer.

7 Weißbier Carousel
One of the quirkier
of the Oktoberfest
drinking spots, this is
the largest mobile bar
on a carousel in the
world – for adults only.

8 Beim Schichtl
Welcome to the
cabaret – this theatre
has been a festival
fixture since 1871.
You can still watch
traditional perform-
ances today, such as
the "beheading" of
an audience member
by the guillotine.

9 Flea Circus
Another old-time
Oktoberfest tradition
not to be missed, these
tiny trained creatures
and their masters have
been entertaining

10 Rides
⏰ 10am–11:30pm
Mon–Thu, 10am–
midnight Fri & Sat
With traditional fair-
ground attractions such
as the merry-go-round
and Ferris wheel, and
adventurous thrill rides,
such as Skyfall, Ketten-
flieger Bayern Tower and
Olympia, there's some-
thing for everyone, from
kids to adults.

Popular Kettenflieger
Bayern Tower ride

NEUSCHWANSTEIN

⬜ Schwangau bei Füssen ⬜ Apr–mid-Oct: 9am–6pm daily; mid-Oct–Mar: 10am–4pm daily ⬜ 1 Jan, 24, 25 & 31 Dec ⬜ neuschwanstein.de ⬜⬜

An idealized vision of a knight's castle on the outside and a homage to Wagner's operas on the inside, Neuschwanstein was Ludwig II's most ambitious project. Around 1.4 million visitors visit Neuschwanstein each year, and it is consequently busy all year round. But don't let this put you off – a day trip from Munich out to Füssen is unmissable.

Ludwig II's oak-panelled bedroom

1 Bedroom
In contrast to the romanticism of the rest of the living quarters, the bedroom is made in Gothic style complete with elaborately carved oak panelling. Scenes from Wagner's *Tristan and Isolde* decorate the walls.

2 Minstrel's Room
The castle's largest room was based on the ceremonial hall of the Wartburg Castle in Eisenach. The walls are adorned with the Legend of Percival.

3 Dining Room
Dishes were transported in a lift from the kitchen three storeys below to the dining room, where the reclusive king took most of his meals, usually on his own. The murals in this predominantly red room depict the tradition of the minstrel's song.

4 Throne Hall
Gold, saints and a touch of Byzantium: the awe-inspiring throne hall is modelled in part after Munich's Allerheiligen-Hofkirche and the Hagia Sophia in Istanbul. This beautiful, church-like ceremonial hall extends over the third and fourth floors – the throne was originally supposed to stand like an altar in the apse. An enormous 4-m- (13-ft-) high chandelier hangs over the hall. Other highlights include the cupola, which is adorned with stars, and the floor mosaic which depicts the earth.

5 Winter Garden
Adjoining the grotto, the Winter Garden affords a spectacular view of the Allgäu region through its large windows.

The magnificent setting of Neuschwanstein

The castle of Hohenschwangau

TOP TIP

Entry to the castle is via guided tours only. Wheelchair users should book in advance.

6 Chapel
The chapel's altar and murals depict Louis IX, the beatified monarch of France and namesake of Ludwig II, king of Bavaria.

7 The Building
Construction of this stunning building began in 1868, with the foundation stone being laid in 1869. The gatehouse was completed first in 1873 and the palace was finished in 1884. Work continued, with the king constantly altering plans, until his death.

The keep and knight's bath were never finished.

8 Hohen-schwangau
Ludwig spent part of his childhood and youth in this summer palace, which is set in wildly romantic scenery.

9 Study
Ludwig's fascinating study features finely carved beams and is filled with murals from Wagner's opera *Tannhäuser*. In the

centre of the room is the king's beautiful desk, which has a fanciful writing set depicting the legend of *Lohengrin*.

10 Grotto
Moving between the living room and study, visitors pass through a small grotto, where a waterfall flowed during the king's lifetime. The larger Venus grotto, complete with a pretty artificial lake, is located in the park of Schloss Linderhof *(p133)*.

TOP 10 OF EVERYTHING

Gingerbread heart souvenirs

PLACES OF WORSHIP

church north of the Alps, and has the second-largest barrel vault in the world after St Peter's in Rome. Its crypt contains the sarcophagi of Elector Maximilian I and Ludwig II. Look out for the bronze figure of St Michael battling the dragon, dating from 1585, on the east façade.

1 Frauenkirche
The twin towers of Munich's 15th-century cathedral (p87) dominate the city's skyline.

2 Michaelskirche
St Michael's Church (p82) lies right in the heart of Munich's pedestrian zone. Its founder, Duke Wilhelm V, built the church for the Jesuit order, which was active in this area from 1559 onwards. Completed in 1597, it is the largest late Renaissance

3 Asamkirche
Officially known as the Church of St John of Nepomuk (p81), this late Baroque structure was designed, financed and built in the 18th century by the Asam brothers. It is located between two houses, one of which belonged to the Asams, and features opulent ceiling frescoes depicting the eponymous saint.

4 Theatinerkirche
The Theatinerkirche (p88) on Odeonsplatz stands out from the crowd with its ochre façade and pure white interior. Construction of this church, which is also called St Cajetan, began in 1663 to mark

Opulent interior of Michaelskirche

Twin-towered façade of the Theatinerkirche

the birth of the heir to Elector Ferdinand. It is the most Italianate of all the churches in Munich.

5 Ludwigskirche

This church (p101), built by Friedrich von Gärtner between 1829 and 1843, is flanked by twin towers built in the Italian Romanesque style. The interior features the expansive *The Last Judgment* fresco by Peter von Cornelius, which is the second-largest church fresco in the world and is definitely worth a visit.

6 Peterskirche

Dating from the 13th century, this is the oldest parish church (p80) in the city, affectionately known as 'Alter Peter' (Old Peter). Its interior is an eclectic mix of Gothic, Baroque and Rococo styles. Brave the 302 steps to the top of the Renaissance tower for superlative views over the Old Town.

7 Synagoge Ohel Jakob

Munich's main synagogue Ohel Jakob ("Jacob's tent") (p80), in Sankt-Jakobs-Platz, forms part of the city's Jewish centre, together with its Jewish Museum and the Israelite Community of Munich. Dating from 2006, its cube-shaped building is crowned with a glass structure and a bronze metallic grid that allows light to flood in. Its sturdy construction, with its irregular, unpolished stonework, is reminiscent of the Western Wall in Jerusalem. Visits are by prearranged tour only; book ahead via the website.

8 Klosterkirche St Anna

🅿 P3 🅐 St-Anna-Straße 19
🕐 6am–7pm daily

The Lehel district is home to Munich's earliest Rococo church, Klosterkirche, which was built by Johann Michael Fischer in 1727–33. The church's interior design can be attributed mainly to the Asam brothers. Right opposite is the grand Neo-Romanesque Pfarrkirche St Anna (p112), which was inspired by the imperial cathedrals of the Rhineland. Constructed much later in 1887–92, its interior is decorated with stunning 18th- and early 19th-century paintings.

9 Damenstiftskirche St Anna

🅿 M3–4 🅐 Damenstiftstraße 1
🕐 8am–8pm daily

Originally a convent for the Sisters of the Salesian Order in the Hacken quarter of Munich's Old Town, St Anna's church is now a school. The late Baroque building dates from 1735, and both the façade and the interior were designed by the Asam brothers. After the church's destruction in World War II, its frescoes were recreated in sepia.

10 Heiliggeistkirche

This lovely church (p82) on Viktualienmarkt is one of the oldest in Munich. The 13th century saw the construction of a hospital church on this site, followed by a Gothic basilica in 1392. In 1724, it was remodelled in Baroque style. The interior blends Gothic and late Baroque with stucco work by the Asam brothers.

HISTORICAL LANDMARKS

of local stone quarries, the interior is a grand affair with a 10-m (330-ft) nave that can hold 20,000 people. The cathedral remained largely unchanged until World War II, when it suffered heavy damage from bombing raids.

4 Olympiapark
Stretching over a vast 85 hectares (210 acres), the park used for the 1972 Olympics, today called Olympiapark (*p40*), offers visitors the chance to live out their Olympic dreams. Go for a swim in the swimming pool, hit the boating lake to practise your rowing or venture into the new Ice Sports Center.

5 Theatinerkirche
Next to the Feldherrnhalle (*p89*) is this gorgeous Rococo church, dating back to the 18th century. The church was initially conceived as an offering of gratitude by Elector Ferdinand Maria for the birth of his son Max Emanuel, the heir to the throne. It was badly damaged by World War II bombing, but extensive work in the decade after the war restored it to its former glory.

1 Neues Rathaus (New Town Hall)
Dominating the city's main square, Marienplatz (*p22*), this Gothic Revival town hall (*p23*) is one of the city's most impressive buildings. Intricate carvings on the façade depict historic figures and events, while the famous Glockenspiel (*p23*) tells stories from Munich's history. The balcony has also become famous as a place where Bayern Munich football team celebrates its successes.

2 Feldherrnhalle
The original purpose of this notable structure on the Odeonsplatz (*p89*) was to serve as a monument to Bavarian military power, with statues of military leaders in the arcades. But it took on a darker meaning under the Nazis. It was the location of Hitler's failed 1923 coup d'état, and he converted the site into a guarded monument to the Nazis killed that night. Only after Hitler's downfall was it restored to its former purpose.

3 Frauenkirche
This Gothic cathedral (*p24*) is possibly the city's most famous land-mark. Built out of bricks due to a lack

Façade of the Maximilianeum, Bavaria's parliament

Bronze memorial to the White Rose movement

6 White Rose Memorial

🗺 F3 📍Geschwister-Scholl-Platz 1

Embedded into the pavement outside the entrance to the Ludwig-Maximilians-Universität *(p101)* is a touching memorial to the White Rose movement, a group of students who resisted the Nazis. Bronze pamphlets are scattered over the pavement, depicting the moment that Sophie Scholl, leader of the group, is said to have thrown her anti-Nazi leaflets, upon seeing the Gestapo arriving to arrest her.

7 City Gates

Between 1285 and 1347, a great defensive wall was constructed to protect the fledgling town of Munich, with four grand entrances. The wall and one of the towers are long gone, demolished in the 18th century, but three gateways to Munich's medieval heart remain: Karlstor, Isartor and Sendlinger Tor *(p82)*. None serves a strategic purpose, but each is worth studying to appreciate the varying architecture of the wall.

8 Siegestor

This magnificent victory gate *(p101)*, reminiscent of the Arc de Triomphe in Paris, was built to honour the glory of the Bavarian army following its victory over Napoleon Bonaparte. After World War II its meaning would be transformed into a memorial for peace.

9 Synagogue Ohel Jakob

Though it may be a newer building, the Ohel Jakob Synagogue *(p80)* is still an important historical landmark due to the context behind it. It was built to replace the old Ohel synagogue that was destroyed by the Nazis during Kristallnacht, the pogrom against Jews. The building is a notable design, made up of two cubes, one atop the other. Inside, glass panels include the names of Munich's Jews killed during Nazi rule.

10 Maximilianeum

The regal Maximilianeum *(p109)* is a stunning piece of Renaissaince-inspired 19th-century architecture. Though it's the seat of the Bavarian Parliament today, the building was initially a school for those from poorer backgrounds, and former students include the once-Bavarian President Franz Josef Strauss and the winner of the Nobel Prize for Physics, Werner Heisenberg.

MUSEUMS AND GALLERIES

1 Städtische Galerie im Lenbachhaus

Lenbachhaus (p95) – once the villa and studio of master painter Franz von Lenbach – contains a collection of works from the famous Blue Rider group. The expanded, renovated complex also holds a large collection of 19th-century German art, while its 20th-century works include artists' rooms, photography, and installations and sculptures by Joseph Beuys.

2 Deutsches Museum

There's fun for the young and old at this science and engineering museum filled with fascinating exhibits (p34).

3 Bayerisches Nationalmuseum

With its cultural and historical exhibits, the national museum (p102) is one of the largest of its kind in Europe. Collections include Gothic sculptures, wall hangings and clocks. The folklore area has a collection of cribs.

Medieval armour, Bayerisches Nationalmuseum

4 Pinakotheken

Known as the Pinakotheken, the Alte (p97) and Neue Pinakothek and the Pinakothek der Moderne (p96) house the city's major art collections. The nearby Museum Brandhorst (p96) is also worth a visit.

5 Bier- und Oktoberfestmuseum

Housed in one of the city's oldest buildings, this museum (p82) covers both the history of beer and the Oktoberfest (p42), telling the story of how the festival is an important part of Munich's tradition. Visitors can sample some of the city's celebrated beers and learn how beer was first made in ancient Egypt, as well as how the beer-making process developed in Munich itself.

6 Glyptothek and Staatliche Antikensammlungen

The exquisite collection of Greek and Roman sculptures and bas-reliefs at the Glyptothek (p95) includes 2,500-year-old gable sculptures from the temple of Aphaea, whose original colouring has been restored. The Antikensammlungen (p95) has antique jewellery, bronzes and Greek ceramics on display.

Artworks, Staedtische Galerie
im Lenbachhaus

7 Jüdisches Museum München

This museum *(p80)* reflects the breadth of Jewish history, art and culture in Munich, and hosts a series of special exhibits.

8 MUCA

A small but carefully curated space *(p80)*, the Museum of Urban and Contemporary Art (MUCA) features works by internationally renowned artists, such as Damien Hirst.

9 Haus der Kunst

Opened in 1937 as an art gallery dedicated to Nazi-approved art, the Haus der Kunst *(p102)* is now used to showcase temporary and travelling art exhibitions.

10 BMW Museum

Considered one of the best car museums in Germany, BMW has a great collection of classic vintage vehicles. Housed in a giant metallic bowl, this brilliant museum *(p126)* features architecture as bold as the cars and motorbikes inside. Vehicles ranging from the earliest models to the boxy cars of the 1980s are on display.

Futuristic bowl-shaped BMW Museum

TOP 10 OTHER MUSEUMS AND GALLERIES

Staatliches Museum Ägyptischer Kunst

1. Staatliches Museum Ägyptischer Kunst
Art from Egypt is the main attraction at this museum *(p96)*.

2. Sammlung Schack
This collection *(p102)* showcases 19th-century masterpieces from the German art world, including works by Von Böcklin, Spitzweg and Schwind.

3. Deutsches Theatermuseum
🅾 N2 🅰 Galeriestraße 4a
Located in the Hofgarten arcades, the Deutsches Theatermuseum covers the history of German theatre.

4. Paläontologisches Museum
Archaeopteryx bavarica, a prehistoric bird, is a highlight at this site *(p98)*.

5. Valentin Karlstadt Musäum
Browse curios relating to Karl Valentin and his sidekick, Liesl Karlstadt, here *(p82)*.

6. Archäologische Staatssammlung
Explore prehistoric, Roman and medieval exhibits here *(p105)*.

7. Alpines Museum
A museum *(p110)* dedicated to the mountains, with a garden exhibit.

8. Museum Fünf Kontinente
This museum *(p110)* has hosted global cultural exhibits since 1926, including the oldest kayak in North America.

9. Kunsthalle
Contemporary art exhibitions are on display at the Kunsthalle *(p90)*.

10. Lothringer 13
🅾 G6 🅰 Lothringer Straße 13
Modern multimedia is on display in this converted factory.

PARKS AND GARDENS

1 Englischer Garten

The Englischer Garten (p32) is a recreational paradise in the city. Every summer, thousands flock to lounge on its lawns; cycle, jog or skate around its many pathways, or sail a boat on the Kleinhesseloher lake. For a spot of refreshment, enjoy a cold brew in one of the park's four beer gardens.

2 Alter Botanischer Garten

The former Botanischer Garten (p127) was once located in this small park, which was also home to the 1854 Glaspalast before it burned down in 1931. Conveniently located near the pedestrian zone between Stachus and the Hauptbahnhof, it now serves as the perfect oasis for relaxing after a shopping spree.

3 Schlosspark Nymphenburg

Enclosed by a wall, this 2-km-(1-mile-) wide park (p38) stretches to the west from the Nymphenburg palace. Various picturesque pavilions and follies are scattered throughout the park, which has been declared a nature reserve to protect its 300-year-old trees.

4 Westpark

Westpark (p118) was created in 1983 for the International Horticultural Exposition. An area of 72 ha (178 acres) was landscaped with numerous artificial hills, pathways, a lake and ponds. The lakeside stage hosts concerts and plays and screens films in summer.

5 Bavariapark

This small park (p117), which lies directly behind the Bavaria statue, was established between 1826 and 1831. Today, it is a great spot to take a break from the hustle and bustle of the city.

6 Hofgarten

The Hofgarten (p88) on the north side of the Residenz (p26) was created in the style of Italian Renaissance gardens. Bounded on two sides by long arcades, it has rows of linden, chestnut and maple trees that provide welcome shade for boules players in the summer. On balmy summer evenings, tango

Mannerist Temple of Diana in the Hofgarten

aficionados meet up for dancing at the Temple of Diana, a 12-sided pavilion that is topped with a shallow dome and located in the centre of the park.

7 Luitpoldpark

Created in celebration of Prince Regent Luitpold's 90th birthday in 1911, this park *(p105)* was extended in 1950 to include the Luitpoldhügel, a hill built out of rubble. From here there's a fine view of the city – on clear days, you can see all the way to the Alps.

8 Hirschgarten

The wild deer enclosure in this garden *(p126)* is a reminder of its former function as a hunting park for the nobility. The park is now popular among lovers of recreational sports, and its beer garden is said to be the largest in the world.

9 Isarauen and Rosengarten

⊠ E6 ⊡ Summer: 8am–8pm daily; winter: 9am–4pm daily
A long stretch of the Isarauen river meadows forms another of Munich's welcome green spaces. South of the

Wittelsbach Bridge is the rose garden, an oasis of tranquillity in the busy city. The small complex also includes an aromatic garden, a garden with poisonous plants and a touch garden for the visually impaired.

10 Botanischer Garten

Created in Schlosspark Nymphenburg in 1914, this *(p125)* is one of the most important botanical gardens in the world. Some 14,000 plant species from around the globe are cultivated here.

Cactus greenhouse at the Botanischer Garten

SPORTS AND ACTIVITIES

1 Bouldering
Bouldering is a form of rock climbing performed without the use of ropes or harnesses. Munich has a handful of bouldering halls throughout the city.

2 Curling
Bavarian curling – also known as ice stock sport – has a long tradition in Munich. It involves competitors sliding ice stocks over an ice surface and is frequently played in the city's beer gardens during winter.

3 Rock Climbing
Munich is an ideal spot for fans of climbing; after all, the Alps are practically on its doorstep. The city is home to a number of artificial climbing walls *(kbthalkirchen.de)* for practising on before heading into the great outdoors to try out a real rock face.

4 Jogging
Munich has parks of all sizes that are perfect for jogging *(p54)*. The most beautiful paths are to be found in the Englischer Garten and along the banks of the Isar. If you prefer not to jog on your own, contact the local organization Roadrunners *(mrrc.de)*, which can put you in touch with a group of runners at your level.

5 Golf
Golf is popular in Munich and the surrounding area, so much so that golfers can choose from more than 40 golf courses *(muenchen-spielt-golf.de)* dotted in and around the Bavarian capital.

ALLIANZ ARENA

The Allianz Arena in Fröttmaning, northern Munich, was built for the World Cup in 2006. Designed by architects Herzog & de Meuron, it has a transparent façade that can be illuminated in numerous colours. Holding 67,000 spectators, the stadium includes an enormous food court. Allianz Arena can be reached via U-Bahn line U6.

6 Football
There are plenty of green spaces in Munich, but if you fancy a spontaneous kick-about with like-minded amateur footballers, Celebreak *(celebreak.com)* helps you get set up. Football lovers can also tour the FC Bayern Museum in the Allianz Arena. The arena often hosts football games, so make sure to check the website *(allianz-arena.com)* in advance for match days.

7 Hiking
There are plenty of beautiful hiking trails in and around Munich that make

Hikers admiring the view of the Zugspitze

for easy walking. If you prefer a more extreme challenge, take a trip to the nearby Alps for mountain hiking. For information on the best routes, contact an organization like the Deutscher Alpenverein *(alpenverein.de)*.

8 Cycling

Home to one of the best cycling path networks in Europe, Munich has several green routes that you can follow without the nuisance of exhaust fumes and noise. Check with the ADFC (German Cyclist's Association; *adfc-bayern.de*) for a variety of cycling tours in and around Munich.

9 Watersports

Munich and the nearby lake regions are a haven in summer for anyone who enjoys swimming, rowing, sailing, windsurfing or canoeing. Destinations range from city swimming pools, which are maintained by SWM *(swm.de)*, to quarry ponds, small, idyllic moor lakes and the great lakes of Upper Bavaria.

10 Winter Sports

The city and its environs are a hub for winter sports fans, whether you like skiing, ice skating, snow-boarding, curling or sledging *(winter-muenchen. de)*. With such a wide variety of winter sports, there's something for everyone.

TOP 10 EVENTS AND TEAMS

BMX rider, Munich Mash

1. Munich Mash
Late Jun Ⓦ munich-mash.com
See the pros performing stunts at Olympiapark.

2. BMW Open
Apr/May Ⓦ bmwopen.de
This tennis tournament is held at the MTTC Iphitos club.

3. BMW International Open
Jun Ⓦ bmw-golfsport.com
The annual golf tournament often takes place in the city.

4. Vierschanzentournee
New Year Ⓦ vierschanzen tournee.com
The best-known ski jump tournament in the world.

5. Isarschwimmen
First day of Oktoberfest
A traditional swimming event sees brave individuals take to the Isar canal.

6. Munich Marathon
Oct Ⓦ generalimuenchen marathon.de
An annual race through the city.

7. Winter Running
Dec–Feb Ⓦ olympiapark.de
A series of races in Olympiapark on three courses.

8. Harness Racing
All year Ⓦ daglfing.de
Held at the Munich Daglfing racecourse.

9. FC Bayern Munich
Ⓦ fcbayern.com
Germany's world-famous football club.

10. TSV 1860 Munich
Ⓦ tsv1860.de
The city's second football club.

OFF THE BEATEN TRACK

1 Designer U-Bahn Stations

Munich's U-Bahn stations really pack a punch: the Marienplatz mezzanine is painted a rich orange-red; lighting designer Ingo Maurer had some great fun with blue at Münchner Freiheit; and Westfried-hof is awash with red, yellow and blue. Georg-Brauchle-Ring features a whole host of different colours, while the Candidplatz stop is embellished with rainbow effects.

2 Bayerische Volks-sternwarte München

H6 **Rosenheimer Straße 45h** **sternwarte-muenchen.de**

Housed in a former air-raid shelter, this public observatory was established by a group of amateur astronomers after World War II. In addition to the telescopes on the observation platform, it has a planetarium and hosts exhibitions. There are also exciting courses and lectures by astronomers. The observatory offers multiple tours, including an evening tour from 9pm Monday to Friday. There's a special tour for children on Fridays at 5pm.

3 Der Verrückte Eismacher

F3 **Amalienstraße 77** **Daily**

With ice cream flavours ranging from the fairly traditional, such as nutty-chocolate, melon or kiwi lime, to the more unusual – cheese-and-chive, beer or asparagus, for example – this popular parlour offers a long list of extraordinary concoctions that changes on a daily basis.

4 Summer Tango

N2 & P4 **Hofgarten**

The unofficial meeting point of Munich's tango fans is the Temple of Diana in the Hofgarten (p26). The otherwise strict site management allows dancers to take part in salsa (Wed and Sun), swing dance (Sun afternoon) and tango (Fri) sessions.

5 Löwenturm am Rindermarkt

N4 **Rindermarkt 9**

The origins of this 12th-century, 23-m- (75-ft-) high tower are a bit of a mystery. It was presumably part of the town ramparts, but could have also been a water tower.

**Interior of the Candidplatz
U-Bahn station**

Unfortunately, it isn't possible to access the interior to see its ribbed vaults and frescos.

6 Hofgarten Boules

📍 N2 🏛 Hofgarten (north side)

The Hofgarten has been a popular meeting point for boules players for over 40 years. When the weather is good, they flock to the park to play, lending it a Mediterranean atmosphere. There's a boules tournament held here every July, but you can watch players enjoying a game throughout the summer months.

7 Gans am Wasser

📍 C6 🏛 Mollsee in Westpark
🕐 Hours vary, check website
🌐 gansamwasser.de

This rustic café is a popular meeting place for locals all year round. Delicious food, such as kebabs and bratwurst rolls, is served alongside a variety of beers. The café is located on the banks of the Mollsee and also hosts music events and

**Patrons at the outdoor
Gans am Wasser**

yoga sessions. Reservations are recommended for larger groups.

8 Olympia-Alm

📍 E1 🏛 Martin-Luther-King-Weg 8 🕐 Noon–midnight daily

The highest beer garden in Munich perches on top of the Olympiaberg at 564 m (1,850 ft). Originally just a kiosk to serve the workers constructing the Olympic Park in 1972, it now offers beer and a selection of hearty Bavarian fare, including Glühwein in winter.

9 Fräulein Grüneis

📍 P2 🏛 Lerchenfeldstraße 1a
🕐 8am–6pm daily

On the banks of the Eisbach in the Englischer Garten, not far from where the surfers hang out, there was once a little toilet block. It was then transformed into a pleasant café kiosk serving exclusively organic goodies, including coffee, sandwiches and cakes. Hot lunch dishes are served daily.

10 Bronze Model of the City

📍 M3 🏛 Frauenplatz

The Frauenkirche serves as the backdrop for this bronze model of Munich's old town, created by Egbert Broerken in 2005. Not only does it help those with visual impairments to find their bearings, but it provides a wonderfully tactile and visual experience for all.

FAMILY ATTRACTIONS

1 FC Bayern Museum

⌂ Werner-Heisenberg-Allee 25
🕐 10am–6pm Mon–Sat (chech website for match day hours)
🌐 fcbayern.com/museum 🔲🔲

This museum attached to the famous football club (p56) is filled with memorabilia and interactive exhibits that will appeal to kids of all ages. Younger kids will love building a stadium with LEGO and making their own versions of famous trophies, while older kids can test their prowess on the indoor pitch or at the skills challenge.

2 BMW Welt

A surefire hit with a younger car-obsessed audience, BMW's mega showroom (p126) lets you get behind the wheel of high-powered models, find out how a petrol engine works and watch motorbike riders perform stunts on the steps and floor space. There's also a café and a shop.

3 Kindermuseum München

📍 E4 ⌂ Arnulfstraße 3 🕐 2–5pm Tue–Fri, 10am–5pm Sat, Sun, public & school hols 🌐 kindermuseum-muenchen.de 🔲

This children's museum offers interactive exhibits, workshops and plenty of games to keep little ones occupied.

4 Olympiapark

The Olympiapark features a jam-packed programme that is the best in the city. Kids who enjoy sport will love the range of activities on offer at the Olympic Park (p40), whether it's in the aquatic centre, beach volleyball court, ski slope, boat centre or streetball court.

5 Deutsches Museum

Older children will be fascinated by the displays at this museum (p34). It has interactive exhibits allowing children to experience physics first hand. They're sure to enjoy both the Technisches Spielzeug (Technical Toys) section and the planet walk from the sun to Pluto, which takes around an hour. Younger children (3–8 years) will enjoy the Kids' Kingdom, where they can learn about science and technology through various hands-on exhibitions. There's also a marble run, night sky and shadow theatre.

6 Bavaria Filmstadt

⌂ Bavariafilmplatz 7 🕐 Open Mar–Oct: 9am–6pm daily; Nov–Feb: 10am–5pm daily 🌐 filmstadt.de 🔲🔲

Film and television productions are still made at these studios. Expect explosions and excitement at the stunt show, and check out the special effects studio to find out how the seemingly impossible is brought to life. At Bullyversum, German film director and actor Michael "Bully" Herbig welcomes every visitor (almost) personally. The 4D experience cinema (children taller than 1.2 m/4 ft only) should not be missed.

Puppet stage at the Marionettentheater

7 Marionettentheater
F4 · **Blumenstraße 32** · **muema-theater.de**

Munich's oldest puppet theatre, founded in 1858, is housed in a small gabled and colonnaded temple dating back to 1900. Performances, enthusiastically received by young and old alike, change frequently, and can range from children's mysteries to *The Magic Flute*.

8 Sea Life
E1 · **Willi-Daume-Platz 1** · **10am–7pm daily** · **visitsealife.com**

Many of the creatures at this aquarium (*p127*) within the Olympiapark are on the Red List of Threatened Species. The seahorses and touch pool are firm favourites with kids, while everyone enjoys feeding time.

9 Wildpark Poing
Osterfeldweg 20, Poing · **9am–4pm daily (Apr–Oct: to 5pm daily)** · **wildpark-poing.net**

A circular route guides visitors on a journey of discovery featuring native species, enclosures and aviaries in a simulated natural habitat. There's the opportunity to feed some of the animals, and birds of prey shows take place in summer.

10 Schauburg
Housed in a former cinema, this theatre (*p55*) for children puts on around 350 performances a year, all in German.

Colourful carousel in the Olympiapark

TOP 10
CHILD-FRIENDLY CAFÉS AND RESTAURANTS

1. Hirschau
H2 · **Gyßlingstraße 15**
The beer garden here has a perfect view of the fenced play park.

2. Seehaus
Seehaus (*p32*) on the Kleinhesseloher See has boats for hire.

3. Café de Bambini
G2 · **MarktstrStraße 7**
Sip on coffee at this café by the lake, while the kids admire local wildlife.

4. Chinesischer Turm
A nostalgic carousel can be found right next to the beer garden (*p68*).

5. Aumeister
Sondermeierstraße 1
This beer garden has its own adventure playground.

6. Kleine Sportgeister
E3 · **Hiltenspergerstraße 43**
A play area and activity room are available for tiny tots.

7. Kaiser Otto
F6 · **Westermühlstraße 8**
There are babysitters in the Kids Lounge during brunch (Sat & Sun).

8. Hofbräukeller
Q4 · **Innere Wiener Straße 19**
This large play area offers supervision for children aged eight and under.

9. Vits
F5 · **Rumfordstraße 49**
A popular coffee roasting house, Vits has a cosy family corner.

10. Zuckertag
E6 · **Ehrengutstraße 10**
Enjoy breakfast, lunch or cake while the little ones have fun in the playroom.

Baked treats, Zuckertag

PERFORMANCE VENUES

1 Isarphilharmonie
The concert hall in the Gasteig HP8 cultural centre, which opened in 2021, can hold around 1,900 visitors. It will serve as the alternative quarters for the Isar Philharmonic until the renovation of the Gasteig *(p110)* is complete.

2 Herkulessaal
N3 **Residenzstraße 1** (Hofgarten entrance) **(089) 290671**
This vast hall within the Residenz hosts a diverse range of concerts, from orchestral pieces to chamber music performances.

3 Deutsches Theater
L3–4 **Schwanthaler-straße 13** **deutsches-theater.de**
The German Theatre is the main venue for hit international musicals such as *Cats*, *Grease*, *Evita* and *West Side Story*, all translated into German, of course.

4 Bavarian State Opera
Run by artistic director Nikolaus Bachler and general musical director Kirill Petrenko, the opera house *(p87)* at the beautiful national theatre draws in half a million visitors every year to over 400 performances.

5 Prinzregententheater
H4 **Prinzregentenplatz 12** **theaterakademie.de**
Built in 1901 as a Wagner festival theatre, the space – conceived as an amphitheatre – is chiefly used as a performance venue for the Bayerische Theaterakademie August Everding.

6 Cuvilliés-Theater
Munich's most elaborate and historically significant theatre *(p27)* is housed in the historic Residenz palace. The venue underwent substantial renovations around around a decade ago and is used for performances by the Bayerische Staatstheater and occasionally for other musical events.

7 Münchner Volkstheater
E6 **Tumblingerstraße 29** **muenchner-volkstheater.de**
Theatregoers come to the "people's theatre" for a sophisticated repertoire of entertaining, popular plays. The Volkstheater has existed and hosted

A musical production at the Deutsches Theater

Rococo and Baroque Cuvilliés Theatre inside the Residenz

shows since 1903, but has been rebuilt several times in that period, most recently in 1983. In 2021 a grand new performance hall was added to the site.

8 Residenztheater

In 1951, the Neues Residenztheater *(p89)* opened its doors next to the opera house. Known as the "Resi", this theatre puts on a wide range of productions across its venues, which include the Cuvilliés-Theater and Marstall.

9 Münchner Kammerspiele

📍 N3 📌 Maximilianstraße 28
🌐 muenchner-kammerspiele.de

Built by Richard Riemerschmid in 1901, this theatre – considered one of the best stages in Germany –became the home of the Münchner Kammerspiele. It caused a stir in the 1920s by staging the works of Bertolt Brecht.

10 Staatstheater am Gärtnerplatz

📍 F5 📌 Gärtnerplatz 3
🌐 gaertnerplatztheater.de

Built in 1865 as a bourgeois equivalent to the royal theatre houses, this intimate theatre hosts operas, operettas and musicals. It opened in late 2017 after renovation.

TOP 10
SMALL STAGES AND CABARETS

1. Metropoltheater
📌 Floriansmühlstraße 5, Freimann
📞 (089) 3219 5533
This is an exceptional alternative theatre with regular performances by the Bavarian Theatre Academy.

2. Komödie im Bayerischen Hof
📍 M3 📌 Promenadeplatz 6
📞 (089) 292810
Enjoy comedies and revues at this theatre in the Bayerischer Hof *(p63)*.

3. HochX
📍 F6 📌 Entenbachstraße 37
📞 (089) 2097 0321
Art and music shows are held here.

4. TamS-Theater
📍 G2 📌 Haimhauserstraße 13a
📞 (089) 345890
This theatre has been hosting unusual productions since 1970.

5. Teamtheater
📍 N4 📌 Am Einlass 2a and 4
📞 (089) 260 4333/6636
An independent theatre with two zones: "Tankstelle" & "Salon".

6. Schauburg
📍 F3 📌 Elisabethplatz
🌐 schauburg.net
A renowned stage with performances specifically written for young people.

7. Blutenburgtheater
📍 D3 📌 Blutenburgstraße 35
🌐 blutenburg-theater.de
This is Munich's only mystery theatre, putting on classic "whodunits".

8. Pasinger Fabrik
📌 August-Exter-Straße 1
📞 (089) 8292 9079
Theatre and opera in a cultural centre.

9. Lach- und Schießgesellschaft
📍 G2 📌 Ursulastraße 9
📞 (089) 391997
This traditional cabaret packs a cutting political bite.

10. Theater im Fraunhofer
📍 F5 📌 Fraunhoferstraße 9
📞 (089) 267850
This small stage hosts everything from music to cabaret.

NIGHTS OUT

1 A Night at the Opera

Munich is home to some of the most fabulous opera performances in the world. See the best shows at the annual Munich Opera Festival (staatsoper.de), which has stages at the Nationaltheater (p86), Prinzregententheater (p62) and the Cuvilliés Theatre (Residenzstraße 1). Outside of the festival, both opera and architecture fans should catch a show by the Bavarian State Opera at the Neo-Classical Nationaltheater.

2 Night Clubs

Whether you want to headbang your way through city-centre stalwarts or hop between clubs in the happening Werksviertel district (p112), Munich has a club to suit every taste. Lavish nights out fuelled by champagne and electro music are found at P1 (p1-club.de) while Harry Klein (harrykleinclub.de) is viewed as one of the best club's in the world, attracting an array of talented DJs.

3 Beers in the Garden

Munich is flushed with beer and gardens, so why not combine them and spend evenings in a beer garden? Visit Augustiner-Keller (p128) for a traditional experience with beer served from wooden barrels, or rub shoulders with locals on benches of Hirschgarten (p126), the biggest beer garden in the world.

4 Observatory Stargazing

You don't need to leave the city to see the stars. Munich's observatory (p59) puts on evening tours where guests can look through four giant telescopes. Each of the telescopes are set-up to focus on specific targets, so you're sure to see something different through each. Most tours are in German, but an English tour is run every Monday.

5 Live Music

Munich loves its music and fortunately it has a great many venues perfect for concerts. The IsarPhilharmonie (p62) is where to be for classical concerts thanks to its excellent acoustics, while rock and indie fans are spoilt for choice thanks to spots such as Muffathalle (p65) and Freiheitshalle (p65), both former power stations, and the more laid-back TonHalle (p65).

6 Theatrical Shows

With over 50 professional theatres, Munich has a world-class theatre scene and a smorgasbord of nightly shows. The Residenztheater (p88) is a throwback to the 1950s, when it was built, and hosts everything from iconic Shakespeare to brand-new shows. Performances here often have English surtitles, as they do at the awesome Art Nouveau Kammerspiele (p90), where many iconic German actors have performed as part of the theatre company.

7 Open-air Events

When the weather is warm, the city bursts with wonderful open-air events to enjoy. Visit the sprawling Olympiapark

Patrons enhjoying a drink
in a beer garden

(p40), which hosts everything from open-air cinema shows to concerts by international acts – think Janet Jackson and Justin Timberlake. Or, hear the next big singer at the Artist Jam Summer Festival (summerjam.de) in Westpark.

8 Brewery Tours
Considered the world capital of beer, Munich has plenty of breweries offering a look behind the scenes. Take in the aromas on brewing day at the Paulaner brewery (paulaner-brauhaus. de) or head to the Haderner brewery (haderner.de) to learn about Munich's first organic brewery. Want to enjoy beer with a snack? Then visit Giesinger (giesinger-braeu.de) where beer is paired with local artisanal cheese.

9 Nights at the Museum
Munich has many great museums and fortunately several keep their doors open late once a week, including Haus der Kunst (p102), the Kunsthalle (p90) and the Museum Brandhorst (p96). The city's big event occurs every October with Lange Nacht der Museen, an evening of city-wide late-night openings, with around 90 museums open until 1am. Join the locals and plot your route to visit the best exhibitions; one ticket gets you into everything.

10 Magic Shows
Enjoy magical evenings in a house of illusions and few places are better than the Table Magic Theater (krist-live. de). Sit in amphitheatre-style seating around Alexander Krist as he captivates you with illusions that will have you questioning reality. Also check out Prinzregententheater (p62); it often has shows featuring local magicians.

Playing cards, often
used in tricks

TOP 10
LIVE MUSIC VENUES

1. Muffathalle
🗺 G5 🏠 Zellstraße 4
🌐 muffatwerk.de
One of the city's most beautiful venues, this concert hall rings with eclectic live music and DJ sets.

2. Backstage
🗺 C4 🏠 Reitknechtstraße 6
🌐 backstage.eu
This is the home of alternative and rock music, with a great range of local and international live acts.

3. IsarPhilharmonie
A cavernous space (p62) filled with classical music, and the pop concert.

4. Hercules Hall
🗺 N3 🏠 Residenzstraße 1
📞 89 290671
Louis I's throne room has been converted into a classical concert hall.

5. Milla
🗺 E5 🏠 Holzstraße 28
🌐 milla-club.de
Hear everything from rock and indie to hip-hop and jazz at this venue.

6. TonHalle
🗺 H6 🏠 Atelierstraße 24
📞 89 628344411
Rock lives at this venue known for its great acoustics and two big bars.

7. Zenith
🏠 Lilienthalallee 29
🌐 motorworld.de
This old railway repair shop is now a huge live venue that attracts.

8. Jazzclub Unterfahrt
🗺 G5 🏠 Einsteinstraße 42
🌐 unterfahrt.de
A place devoted to jazz. Performances are by local and international artists.

9. Freiheitshalle
🗺 D4 🏠 Rainer-Werner-Fassbinder-Platz 🌐 backstage.eu
All genres can be heard here. Look out for the 70s or 80s themed nights

10. Einstein Kultur
🗺 G5 🏠 Einsteinstraße 42
🌐 einsteinkultur.de
Once a beer cellar, today this cultural centre has nightly live performances.

BAVARIAN DISHES

1 Münchner Schnitzel
The Wittelsbachs *(p9)* were related to the Habsburgs, and so many of the dishes commonly served in Bavaria were originally inspired by Bohemian Austrian cuisine, for example *Knödel* (dumplings), *Mehlspeisen* (pastries) and even schnitzel. The Munich twist on schnitzel includes a horseradish, sweet mustard and *Breznbrösel* (pretzel breadcrumb) coating.

2 Kässpätzle
A type of soft egg noodle, *Spätzle* originated in the Swabia region. The cooking method involves scraping the almost runny *Spätzle* dough into boiling water. The end product is available in a variety of versions and dishes. One dish, known as *Allgäuer Kässpätzle*, involves cheese and minced onions.

3 Wurst
In Bavaria, *Wurst* (sausage) is eaten as part of a cold snack known as *Brotzeit* ("bread time"). A regional speciality is *Weißwurst* (veal sausage), which is warmed in hot water and peeled out of its skin before being enjoyed with sweet mustard. Typical hot sausage dishes include *Schweinswürstl* (Franconian pork sausages) served with sauerkraut or *Leberkäse* (meat loaf). *Lyoner* (parboiled sausages) are the star of the show in any self-respecting Bavarian *Wurstsalat* (sausage salad).

**Cooking *Steckerlfisch*
on a charcoal grill**

4 Steckerlfisch
Those who have been to Oktoberfest will be more than familiar with the smell of this fish on a stick, typically trout, char or mackerel, cooked on a charcoal grill.

5 Schweinebraten
Succulent *Schweinebraten* (roast pork) is a real Bavarian favourite. The local way to cook it involves scoring the rind before putting the joint into an oven to roast. The meat is then continuously basted with beer (ideally dark lager) while it is roasting, until the rind develops into crispy crackling. *Schweinebraten* is traditionally served with *Knödel* and sauerkraut or coleslaw.

6 Knödel
Dumplings are a mainstay of Bavarian cooking. Originally a means of using up leftover, stale bread rolls by soaking them, *Semmelknödel* are particularly popular. A tasty alternative is the *Breznknödel*, made with stale *Laugenbrezel* (lye pretzels). Another type is *Kartoffelknödel*, made from grated potatoes with a toasted cube of white bread in the centre. Dumplings that are made exclusively from cooked potatoes are also sometimes used for making sweet pastries, such as *Zwetschgen-knödel* (plum dumplings).

**Bratwurst
served with
red cabbage**

7 Brezn and Semmeln
The *Laugenbrezn* is the region's most popular and common type of pretzel, and its appeal skyrockets during Oktoberfest. *Semmel* is the Bavarian name for a bread roll.

8 Obatzda
This spreadable cheese (made from Camembert, butter, quark, paprika and onion) is a beer-garden favourite.

9 Gebäck
The Bavarian region is home to a whole host of *Gebäck* (pastries). Anyone with a sweet tooth should look out for *Zwetschgendatschi* (plum cake), *Rohrnudeln* (sweet filled rolls made from yeast dough) and the ever-popular *Auszogne* (doughnuts).

10 Süßspeisen
Bavarian *Süßspeisen* (desserts) are typically hearty. Favourites include *Apfelstrudel* (apple strudel), *Hollerkücherl* (elderflower pancakes), *Dampfnudeln* (steamed dumplings) and Austrian *Kaiserschmarrn* (shredded pancakes), often served with fruit compote.

Homemade *Apfelstrudel* with walnuts and raisins

TOP 10
VEGETARIAN AND
VEGAN RESTAURANTS

Appetizers at Prinz Myshkin

1. Prinz Myshkin
Munich's top vegetarian restaurant *(p85)* is known for serving imaginative meat-free and vegan dishes.

2. Max Pett
⚑ M4 ⌂ Pettenkoferstraße 8
This place serves plant-based vegan dishes. Alcohol is not available here.

3. Café Ignaz
⚑ E3 ⌂ Georgenstraße 67
An extensive menu featuring crêpes, gnocchi and organic beer.

4. Gratitude
⚑ M4 ⌂ Türkenstraße 55
This organic restaurant offers vegan, gluten-free and raw dishes.

5. Bodhi
⚑ D5 ⌂ Ligsalzstraße 23
Vegan Bavarian-style restaurant serving *Obatzda* and schnitzel burgers.

6. Vegelangelo
⚑ P4 ⌂ Thomas-Wimmer-Ring 15
The vegetarian food here packs a real punch, from the pasta creations to the truffle risotto.

7. NOAMS
⚑ F5 ⌂ Holzstraße 19
A laidback restaurant known for its healthy vegetarian and vegan fare.

8. Deli Kitchen
⚑ L2 ⌂ Augustenstraße 5
A vegan shop with its own small stylish restaurant.

9. Tushita Teehaus
⚑ F5 ⌂ Klenzestraße 53
Great teas and fresh vegan snacks.

10. Lost Weekend
⚑ E3 ⌂ Schellingstraße 3
A popular bookshop café serving vegan coffee and cake.

BEER GARDENS

1 Taxisgarten

This neighbourhood beer garden (p128) in Neuhausen is sheltered by ash and chestnut trees. A popular meeting place, it can seat up to 1,500 guests.

2 Augustiner-Keller

This vast beer garden (p128) shaded by ancient chestnut trees and located near a former place of execution has been in operation since the 19th century. There are 5,000 seats for guests, of which half have table service. About 200 decorated tables for the regulars add a whimsical note. There is also a play area. On warm summer evenings, this beer garden is packed. Don't miss the Augustiner Edelstoff on tap from wooden barrels.

3 Chinesischer Turm

With 7,000 seats, the Chinese Tower (p33) is one of the city's most famous landmarks, and is frequented by students, tourists and locals alike. Brass bands play on the first floor of the pagoda at the weekend. There is also a play area and an old wooden carousel nearby.

4 Seehaus

A great place to people-watch, this popular beer garden (p32) is at the centre of the Englischer Garten,

right on the Kleinhesseloher See. It can accommodate 2,500 people, with 400 more on the stylish terrace. The beer garden (serving Paulaner) has a cosy atmosphere. Boats can be hired by the lake. There is also a play area.

5 Hofbräukeller

🚇 Q4 🏠 Innere Wiener Straße 19

Across the Isar in Haidhausen, the Hofbräukeller – once the site of a brewery and its cellar – has been serving beer since 1892. There are 1,400 tables, of which 400 have table service. The dense canopy of chestnuts keeps drinkers comfortable and dry even on damp days. There is also a play area on the premises.

6 Aumeister

🏠 Sondermeierstraße 1

This huge beer garden (3,000 capacity) on the north side of the Englischer Garten serves Hofbräu, along with a selection of seasonal beers, including Starkbier in March, and Sommerbier and Wiesnbier during Oktoberfest. Parasols shelter drinkers on the Mediterranean terrace. There is also an adventure playground here.

Relaxing in the tranquil setting of Seehaus

Enjoying a chilled beer in Hirschgarten

7 Hirschgarten

Munich's largest beer garden (*p126*) seats 8,000 people and is next to Schloss Nymphenburg. Augustiner Edelstoff is served on tap from the huge wooden barrel, known as a "Hirsch".

8 Wirtshaus am Bavariapark

Chestnut trees shelter this beer garden and pub (*p123*) in Bavariapark with capacity for 1,200 patrons (and a further 300 on the terrace). Augustiner is served here.

9 Biergarten am Viktualienmarkt

N4 **Viktualienmarkt 9**

Nestled between the market stalls of Viktualienmarkt, this centrally located beer garden seats 800 people, with table service for 200. It serves beer from all of Munich's breweries on a six-week rotation. In the summer months, it hosts concerts by traditional bands on Sundays, and the Brunnenfest takes place on the first Friday in August.

10 Zum Flaucher

E6 **Isarauen 8**

This idyllic beer garden (700 capacity) on the banks of the Isar is dotted with beautiful old trees. You're likely to come across sunbathers on the Isar beach, as well as cyclists and families with children (the garden has a play area). Löwenbräu is offered here.

TOP 10
BAVARIAN BEERS

1. Augustiner
Brewed since 1328 in the monastery near the cathedral, under the purity law of 1516, Augustiner is regarded as the champagne of beers.

2. Andechser
Beer has been brewed at this Benedictine abbey on the "sacred mountain" since the Middle Ages.

3. Paulaner
Pauline monks in the Au began to brew beer as far back as 1634. The most famous master brewer was Brother Barnabas. Salvator beer is still made using his 18th-century recipe.

4. Löwenbräu
Dating back to the 14th century, this is made in Munich's largest brewery.

5. Hofbräu
Duke Wilhelm V founded his own court brewery in 1589. A new fermenting site was set up on Platzl in 1607 – it is now known as the Hofbräuhaus.

6. Spaten
This brewery is named after the 16th-century Spatt family.

7. Hacker-Pschorr
The first recorded mention of this beer was in 1417. Today, it is part of the Paulaner Group.

8. Erdinger Weißbier
Erdinger is one of the top sellers among nearly 1,000 different types of Bavarian wheat beers.

9. Ayinger
This small brewery in Aying is home to a dozen well-known beers.

10. Franziskaner Weissbier
Franciscan friars have brewed this beer since 1363 in the former monastery on Residenzstraße. Now part of the Spaten-Löwenbräu Group.

Franziskaner Weissbier beer

TRADITIONAL TAVERNS

Traditional Bavarian pub, Zum Franziskaner

1 Zum Franziskaner
N3 **Residenzstraße 9**
zum-franziskaner.de
This 200-year-old traditional pub is said to serve the best *Leberkäse* (meat loaf) in town. The *Weißwürste* (sausages) are highly recommended too.

2 Hofbräuhaus
You can't come to Munich and not pay a visit to the most famous beer hall *(p87)* in the world.

3 Schneider Bräuhaus
The former Weiße Bräuhaus offers traditional Munich fare, including delicious *Kronfleischküche* (skirt steak dishes). Whether you opt for *Kalbslüngerl* (pickled lights of veal), *Milzwurst* (spleen sausage) or *Schweinsbraten* (roast pork), the food here *(p85)* is outstanding. A wheat bock beer called Aff is served on tap.

4 Wirtshaus in der Au
G5 **Lilienstraße 51**
wirtshausinderau.de
The Wirtshaus, founded in 1901, is renowned for its dumplings, which include varieties containing either wild garlic, spinach or ham. Meat lovers might also want to try the duck, steak or ox fillet. Renowned dumpling-making courses are run by the owners for locals and visitors alike. Paulaner and Auer craft beer are served on tap.

5 Löwenbräukeller
This historic building *(p98)* complete with an exquisite taproom, a ceremonial hall and a large beer garden dominates the Stiglmaier-platz. It also serves as a venue for carnival balls and congresses, and plays host to the tapping of the first Triumphator barrel to welcome in the "fifth season" in March. A stone lion, the Löwenbräu emblem, sits above the entrance.

6 Spatenhaus an der Oper
N3 **Residenzstraße 12**
kuffler.de/de/spatenhaus
The ground floor of this traditional pub on Max-Joseph-Platz has a homely, unpretentious atmosphere, while the upper floor has a more sophisticated ambience. Diners come here to enjoy a menu of hearty Munich cooking.

Beautiful dining room, Spatenhaus an der Oper

7 Zum Augustiner
Housed in a traditional building that operated as a brewery until 1885, this large restaurant *(p85)* has an interior that's well worth a look (particularly the mussel hall). In summer, there is outdoor seating in the paved pedestrian zone and in an arcaded courtyard.

8 Paulaner Bräuhaus
A cosy, homely pub *(p123)* furnished with dark wood and brewing equipment. House-brewed Paulaner is, of course, served on tap. The game dishes in particular are excellent.

9 Fraunhofer
🚇 F5 🏠 Fraunhoferstraße 9 🌐 fraunhofertheater.de
Parts of this atmospheric tavern date back to when it was first built, in around 1900. It attracts a mix of locals and tourists and hosts weekly music sessions on Sunday mornings. Its courtyard is home to both a cabaret stage and the legendary Werkstattkino cinema.

10 Augustiner Bräustuben
While Oktoberfest is in full swing, this *(p123)* is the place to come for a glimpse of the brewery's show horses. Both the inn itself and the brewery's stables are brimming with traditional Bavarian charm.

TOP 10
MUNICH TRADITIONS

1. Schäfflertanz
Every 7 years 🏙 Munich
This dance of the Schäffler takes place every seven years (next in Jan 2026) to commemorate the end of the plague.

2. Tanz der Marktfrauen
Shrove Tue 🏙 Munich
Women at the Viktualienmarkt stalls dance in colourful costumes.

3. Starkbierzeit
St Joseph's Day (19 Mar) until Easter 🏙 Bavaria
Celebrating the "fifth season of the year" by tapping barrels of potent Starkbier.

4. Maibaum
1 May 🏙 Bavaria
The day to set up the maypole.

5. Fronleichnamsprozession
Thu after Trinity Sunday 🏙 South Bavaria
Processions for the Feast of Corpus Christi take place across South Bavaria, the largest running through Munich.

6. Kocherlball
Third Sun in Jul 🏙 Munich
Enjoy an early morning beer (6–10am) as costumed couples dance the Ländler, Zwiefacher and Polka to pay homage to the servants who once did the same.

7. Sonnwendfeuer
During summer solstice 🏙 Munich
The longest day of the year is celebrated with bonfires in the mountains around Munich. The biggest one is in the Spitzsteinhaus.

8. Christkindlmärkte
Advent until 24 Dec 🏙 Bavaria
Christmas markets around the city.

9. Alphornblasen, Jodeln and Schuhplatteln
Sep 🏙 Bavaria
Alphorns, yodelling and the thigh-slapping Schuhplatteln dance.

10. Leonhardi-Umzüge
First Sunday in Nov 🏙 Upper Bavaria
Processions in honour of St Leonhard, patron saint of horses.

MUNICH FOR FREE

1 Surfers on the Eisbach
The bridge next to the Haus der Kunst usually gets crowded with enthusiastic spectators who come to watch and cheer on the surfers riding the artificial waves created in the Eisbach stream *(p33)* all year round.

2 Gasteig HP8
During the multi-year renovation of the Gasteig *(p110)* in Haidhausen, events – including free concerts, exhibitions, readings and courses – will take place in the Gasteig HP8.

3 Museums and Galleries
The Museum für Abgüsse Klassischer Bildwerke *(Katharina-von-Bora-Straße 10)*, Geologisches Museum *(Luisenstraße 37)*, Kartoffel-museum *(Grafinger Straße 2)*, Feuerwehrmuseum *(An der Hauptfeuerwache 8)* and Lothringer 13 *(p53)* all offer free admission. A number of other major museums (including the Pinakotheken) are also free for under-18s.

4 BMW Welt
The dynamic architecture of this futuristic building *(p126)* with its double cone entrance makes it well worth a visit. Exhibitions are free to enter.

5 Glockenspiel
The famous Glockenspiel *(p23)* chiming clock in the alcoves of the Neues Rathaus springs into action every day at 11am and noon (and again at 5pm in summer). The top section depicts the wedding of Duke Wilhelm V and Renate von Lothringen with a jousting tournament. Beneath them is the coopers' dance.

6 Olympiapark
While many of the attractions at Olympiapark *(p40)* have an entry fee, it doesn't cost a thing to wander the site, admiring the 1970s architecture of various Olympic venues. For fans of fireworks, the Sommernachtstraum (Midsummer Night's Dream) event in July puts on a spectacular display. You can even pack up a picnic and listen from inside the park whenever major concerts take place at the stadium.

Museum für Abgüsse Klassischer Bildwerke

Surfer riding the wave
on the Eisbach

7 Theatron
At Whitsuntide and for three weeks in the summer, free concerts (p75) are held at the amphitheatre in Olympiapark.

8 Training at FC Bayern
Experience a training session with the masters: fans can visit the stadium on Säbener Straße 51 to get up close and personal with their football heroes and maybe even bag an autograph. Dates of public training sessions are available on the club shop's website (fcbayern.com).

9 Forstenrieder Park
Just southwest of Munich, the Forstenrieder Park is a peaceful place for a stroll – and home to dozens of wild boar and deer.

10 Open-Air Performances
The Gärtnerplatztheater orchestra plays a free concert at the Gärtnerplatzfest in July. In summer and autumn, the Mohr-Villa and the amphitheatre on the north side of the Englischer Garten stage classic plays (muenchner-sommer theater.de). "Oper für alle" puts on a live transmission of an opera performance on Max-Joseph-Platz and a free festival concert on Marstallplatz in July.

Open-air concert in
the Gärtnerplatz

TOP 10
BUDGET TIPS

Tram passing Maximilianstraße

1. Sightseeing by Tram
Tram 19 passes by Lenbachplatz, along Maximilanstraße and across the Isar to Haidhausen.

2. CityTourCard
For regular users of public transport, the CityTourCard (p145) also offers discounts on over 60 attractions.

3. Views for Free
Soak up the impressive city views for free from the Friedensengel (p109) or the summit of Olympiaberg (p50).

4. Discovering the City on a Bike
Explore Munich on a budget with MVG Rad (p141), the city's cycle-hire system.

5. Museums for a Euro
The state museums, along with some others, offer entry to the permanent exhibitions for just €1 on Sundays.

6. Sunset on the Terrace
The roof terrace of the Ruby Lilly Hotel (ruby-hotels.com) has a great view and reasonably priced drinks.

7. MVV Group Tickets
The MVV (Munich Traffic and Tariff Association) offers cheap group tickets for up to five adults.

8. District Festivals
Dachau and Rosenheim have popular summer Volksfeste and are a cheaper alternative to the Oktoberfest.

9. Picnic in the Beer Garden
You can take your own snacks to any beer garden and just pay for drinks.

10. Kinotag
For cut-price movie tickets, Kinotag (cinema day) is on Mondays (also Tuesdays in some cinemas).

FESTIVALS AND EVENTS

1 Dance
Every 2 years in May (2025, 2027) W dance-muenchen.de
This innovative dance festival takes place at about ten different venues around the city, including the Deutsches Museum and Residenztheater.

2 Zamanand Festival
May/Jun & Sep W zamanand.de
This sustainability festival takes place over two weekends a year. Leopoldstraße and Ludwigstraße are closed off to traffic as food and drink vendors take over the streets.

3 Münchener Biennale
Every 2 years in May/Jun (2026, 2028) W muenchenerbiennale.de
The first of its kind in the world, this musical theatre festival was founded in 1988 by composer Hans Werner Henze (1926–2012). The city of Munich commissions young composers to write their first full work for the festival.

4 Filmfest
End Jun/early Jul W filmfest-muenchen.de
Smaller than the Berlin festival and not quite as star-studded, Filmfest (p74) is one of Europe's most important film festivals. Held since 1983, it has made a name for itself as a festival of the people.

5 Opernfestspiele
End Jun–end Jul W staatsoper.de/festspiele
Under Ludwig II, Munich grew into a centre of music, and it was the site of premieres of Wagner's operas and of a major Mozart festival. In 1910, the Richard Strauss festival week was launched, a tradition continued in the Opernfestspiele (Munich Opera Festival), which features both classic works and contemporary pieces. Free "Opera for all" performances are also held.

6 Tollwood
Jun/Jul & Nov–New Year W tollwood.de
A popular bi-annual music, dance and theatre festival, held in summer at the Olympiapark South and in winter on the Theresienwiese. Formerly an alternative event, it has matured into a major festival with a wide-ranging programme of performances, vendors and organic foods.

Theatron Musiksommer
in Olympiapark

7 Königsplatz Open Air
Jul & Aug Ⓦ hinoopenair.de
The backdrop of the Königsplatz seems tailor-made for open-air events. In summer, you can enjoy a wide variety of concerts here, ranging from classical to rock and pop. The large square is also used for open-air film screenings.

8 Theatron Musiksommer and PfingstFestival
Whitsun, Aug Ⓦ theatron.de
At Whitsuntide, as well as for 24 days during the summer, the amphitheatre at Olympiapark hosts a variety of musical events. The programme features artists from around the globe, and there's a real laid-back vibe about the whole event.

9 Oktoberfest
Last two weeks in Sep
Ⓦ oktoberfest.de
The largest beer festival in the world (p42) runs in Munich for 16 or 17 days, ending on the first Sunday of October.

10 SpielArt
Every 2 years in Oct & Nov (2025, 2027) Ⓦ spielart.org
Munich's "window on the world of theatre" presents new productions from around the world at various venues, usually with a focus on one country.

Colourful stall at the
Tollwood Winter Festival

TOP 10
OTHER EVENTS

1. Lange Nächte
May & Oct Ⓦ muenchner.de
The "long night" of music is held in the summer; the equivalent event for museums happens later in the year.

2. Frühlingsfest
Mid-Apr–start of May
Folk festival held on the Theresienwiese.

3. DOK.fest München
Watch international documentary films, premieres and work from up-and-coming directors.

4. Stadtgründungsfest
Weekend closest to 2 June
A cultural programme between Marienplatz and Odeonsplatz.

5. Brunnenhofkonzerte
Jun–Aug
Enjoy classical music, tango, movie scores and many other genres at the Residenz on warm summer nights.

6. Krimifestival
Spring and autumn
Ⓦ krimifestival-muenchen.de
International crime thriller authors visit the Isar to perform readings.

7. Christopher Street Day
Jul Ⓦ csdmuenchen.de
Parade and show programme put on by the LGBTQ+ community.

8. Fantasy Filmfest
Horror films, thrillers and more.

9. Stadtteilwochen
Summer, individual districts
Each district puts on its own week-long festival with food and cultural events.

10. BallettFestwoche
Apr Ⓦ bayerische.staatsoper.de
In-house productions by the Staatsballett with guest performances.

Performers at BallettFestwoche

AREA BY AREA

Cathedral of Our Dear Lady

SOUTHERN OLD TOWN

This area is where Munich began in 1158 and remains the beating heart of the city to this day, with many of Munich's best shopping areas and some of its oldest buildings. At its centre is the former grain and salt market of Marienplatz, now the city's main square and a popular meeting place for locals and tourists alike. Much of the area around the square is pedestrianized, making it easy to get around and see the fine historic buildings, including the Frauenkirche and Peterskirche, or the market at the Viktualienmarkt, which has been held here for over 200 years.

1 Neues Rathaus

🔲 N3 🔲 Marienplatz 8 📞 (089) 2339 6555 ⏱ Tower: 10am–7pm Mon–Fri (winter: to 5pm) 🚻♿

The Neo-Gothic New Town Hall was built by Georg Hauberrisser and is home to the mayor's office. Guided tours of the building run on Monday, Friday and Saturday – a lift takes visitors up to the 85-m (279-ft) high observation deck in the tower. At the top of the tower sits the city's mascot, the Münchner Kindl (a young monk). The Rathaus draws a crowd at least twice a day when its Glockenspiel starts to chime (at 11am and noon, also at 5pm in summer).

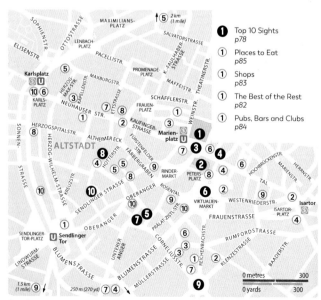

- 🔟 Top 10 Sights p78
- ① Places to Eat p85
- ① Shops p83
- ① The Best of the Rest p82
- ① Pubs, Bars and Clubs p84

0 metres 300
0 yards 300

For places to stay in this area, see p146

Gilded statues adorning the nave at Peterskirche

2 Peterskirche

🗺 N4 🏠 Rindermarkt 1 🕐 Tower: 9am–7pm Mon–Fri, 10am–7pm Sat & Sun (winter: to 6pm) 🌐 alterpeter.de 🔗

The oldest church in the city dates back to the 12th century, although it has undergone a number of stylistic renovations since. A gilded figure of St Peter stands in the middle of the main altar and the remains of St Munditia are on display in a glass coffin. The view from the 91-m (299-ft) high tower is spectacular. You need to pay an extra fee to climb the tower.

3 Marienplatz

Munich's main square *(p22)* is dominated by the Neues Rathaus, while its eastern side is bounded by the Gothic Altes Rathaus. Both the Mariensäule and the Fischbrunnen are popular meeting spots, the latter dating back to the Middle Ages. Every year on Ash Wednesday, the fountain is the site of a traditional ceremony that started back in 1426: Geldbeutel-waschen, when the mayor and city councillors wash empty money bags for good luck. Marienplatz is a hive of activity, playing host to festivals, demonstrations, and FC Bayern celebrations (trophies are presented from the town hall balcony).

4 Altes Rathaus

🗺 N4

Construction of the Gothic Old Town Hall on Marienplatz started in 1470 under architect Jörg von Halspach. The building was the seat of the city council until 1874 and is still a popular venue for official events; its ceremonial hall has a re-constructed barrel vault, adorned with coats of arms. Once the city administration moved to the Neues Rathaus, the ground floor was converted to create a drive-through and a pedestrian passage to Tal. The tower is now a toy museum *(spielzeugmuseummuenchen.de)*.

Gothic façade of the Altes Rathaus on Marienplatz

5 Synagoge Ohel Jakob

⊞ M4 ⬚ St-Jakobs-Platz 18
🌐 ihg-m.de/juedisches-zentrum ⬚

Munich's main synagogue, Ohel Jakob, was unveiled in November 2006. Its design, by architects Wandel Höfer Lorch, features two stacked cubes: a solid travertine base topped with a delicate glass structure and a metallic grid. The synagogue is the jewel in the crown of an ensemble comprising the Jewish Museum and a community centre. Access to the building is via an underground Corridor of Remembrance from the community centre.

6 Viktualienmarkt

⊞ N4 ⬚ 7am–8pm Mon–Sat

Viktualienmarkt exudes a unique atmosphere. This former farmers' market has become a real foodie destination, but it doesn't come cheap. The market has its own beer garden, as well as six fountains featuring local figures. Shrove Tuesday is always a great spectacle, when women come out from their stalls to take part in the famous "Tanz der Marktfrauen" (Dance of the Market Women). At the southernmost end of the market is Der Pschorr restaurant (p85) and the reconstructed Schrannenhalle from 1853, which is home to the popular deli chain, Eataly (Blumenstraße 4).

7 Jüdisches Museum München

⊞ M4 ⬚ St-Jakobs-Platz 16 ⬚ 10am–6pm Tue–Sun 🌐 juedisches-museum-muenchen.de ⬚

This freestanding cube of a museum with its wraparound glazing presents Jewish history and culture in Munich as part of its permanent exhibition, titled "Stimmen – Orte – Zeiten" (Voices – Places – Times). It also puts on temporary exhibitions.

8 MUCA

⊞ M4 ⬚ Hotterstraße 12
⬚ 10am–6pm Wed & Fri–Sun, 10am–8pm Thu 🌐 muca.eu ⬚ ⬚

It isn't widely known beyond the city, but Munich is the birthplace of Germany's thriving graffiti scene. Located in a former substation, close to Asamkirche, this modern museum has a fabulous array of urban and street art by international artists. It also offers tours focusing on street art, including bike tours. Visitors can pre-book admission tickets online from the website.

9 Gärtnerplatz

⬚ F5

This hexagonal square was laid out in 1860 and named to commemorate the German architect Friedrich von Gärtner. Its central fountain and flower beds lend it something of a Mediterranean feel. At the square's

Cube-shaped exterior of the Jüdisches Museum München

southern end is the Neo-Classical Staatstheater am Gärtnerplatz (p63), a theatre dating from 1865. The square now sits right at the heart of the Gärtnerplatz quarter, renowned for its shops, restaurants and numerous cafés. The area is also home to Munich's LGBTQ+ scene, along with the neighbouring Glockenbach quarter.

10 Asamkirche and Asam-Haus

◉ M4 ◘ Sendlinger Straße 32–4
◘ Church: 9am–5pm daily

Between 1729 and 1733, Egid Quirin Asam purchased four separate properties on Sendlinger Straße. This is where he built his extensively stuccoed residence and – together with his brother Cosmas Damian – the Asamkirche (Church of St John of Nepomuk) of 1733. This late Baroque structure was intended to be a private church (it offered a direct view of the high altar from the Asam-Haus), but the city council refused to grant a construction permit until the brothers agreed to make it accessible to the public. Sandwiched between the houses, the church has no surface left unadorned. It overflows with cherubs and barley-sugar columns, false marble and stucco, frescos and oil paintings. The hidden windows of the interior let in only a little light, which evokes an almost mystical atmosphere.

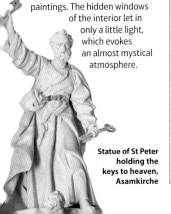

Statue of St Peter holding the keys to heaven, Asamkirche

A DAY IN THE SOUTHERN OLD TOWN

Morning

Start the day with a coffee in **Cotidiano** (Gärtnerplatz 6) with a view of the **Staatstheater am Gärtnerplatz** (p63) and its square. From here, take a stroll down the streets and explore the shops and boutiques of the area. When you reach Rumfordstraße, take a left onto Utzschneiderstraße and you'll see the Schrannenhalle right ahead, which is now a branch of the Italian deli chain, **Eataly** (Blumenstraße 4). You can either buy a snack here, or check out the wide selection on offer at **Viktualienmarkt**. Here you can enjoy lunch in the beer garden, with a great view of the square.

Afternoon

Once you've refuelled, head down Prälat-Zistl-Straße and turn right onto St-Jakobs-Platz to reach the **Jüdisches Museum** and the Münchner Stadtmuseum. Be sure to visit the "Typisch München" (Typical Munich) exhibit at the Stadtmuseum. Next, walk down Oberanger, taking a right turn onto Schmidstraße towards **Sendlinger Straße** (p82). Here, you will find the **Asamkirche** and Asam-Haus. Now head north to **Marienplatz** (p22), where the famous Glockenspiel attraction awaits you at the **Neues Rathaus** (p78) at 5pm (Mar–Oct). Try to find a spot for dinner in one of the busy restaurants along **Tal** or around the Viktualienmarkt.

The Best of the Rest

1. Sendlinger Tor
🅜 M4
This city gate (Stadttor) from 1318 marks the southern entrance to Sendlinger Straße.

2. Isartor
🅜 N4 🅐 Tal 50 🅦 valentin-karlstadt-musaeum.de 🔗
The Valentin-Karlstadt-Musäum in the south tower of the Isartor is devoted to cabaret artists Karl Valentin and Liesl Karlstadt. The Turmstüberl (museum café) is furnished in *fin-de-siècle* style.

3. Bürgersaalkirche
🅜 M3 🅐 Neuhauser Straße 14
The Bürgersaal (community hall) has been used as a church by the Sodality of Our Lady since 1778.

4. Heiliggeistkirche
🅜 N4 🅐 Tal 77 🅦 heilig-geist-muenchen.de
This Viktualienmarkt church is one of the city's oldest.

5. Künstlerhaus
🅜 M3 🅐 Lenbachplatz 8
The Künstlerhaus (House of Artists) on Lenbachplatz was once a meeting place for artists and Munich society. It now hosts cultural events.

6. Karlstor and Stachus
🅜 M3
Karlsplatz/Stachus features fountains and the medieval Karlstor.

7. Michaelskirche
🅜 M3 🅐 Neuhauser Straße 6 🅦 st-michaelmuenchen.de
This Jesuit church is a prime example of Renaissance architecture.

8. Deutsches Jagd- und Fischereimuseum
🅜 M3 🅐 Neuhauser Straße 2 🅦 jagd-fischerei-museum.de 🔗
Hunting and fishing displays, including jackalope-type creations, in the former Augustinerkirche.

9. Bier- und Oktoberfestmuseum
🅜 N4 🅐 Sternecherstraße 2 🅦 bier-und-ohtoberfestmuseum.de 🔗
Housed in a medieval building, this museum presents Munich's history of beer along with everything you need to know about Oktoberfest.

10. Ignaz-Günther-Haus
🅜 M4 🅐 St-Jahobs-Platz 20
This 16th-century late Gothic house was the home and studio of sculptor Ignaz Günther (1725–75).

Distinctive towers of the medieval Isartor

Stores lining the busy Kaufingerstraße

Shops

1. Kauf Dich Glücklich
N4 Reichenbachstraße 14
One of two branches in Munich offering the latest trends from niche clothes designers to well-known brands. Also sells a selection of shoes, music and gifts.

2. Kaufingerstraße and Neuhauser Straße
M3
This pedestrian zone is Munich's biggest shopping street.

3. Nica's Cosmos
N4 Müllerstraße 1
This store is brimming with many children's items that have been lovingly selected, including organic children's and baby clothes from boutique design workshops, innovative and educational toys, and much more.

4. Globetrotter
N4 Isartorplatz 8–10
Lovers of the great outdoors need to look no further: everything you could possibly want or need is right here, along with a canoe-testing pool, cold room, a climbing wall and a children's play area.

5. HOFSTATT
M4 Sendlinger Straße 10
Once the home of the *Süddeutsche Zeitung* newspaper, this shopping mall has its own inner courtyards and sells fashion, accessories, cosmetics and food.

6. Ludwig Beck
N3 Marienplatz 11
Also known as "Store of the Senses", this shop is in a league of its own for fashion, lingerie, stationery and music.

7. Blutsgeschwister
F5 Gärtnerplatz 6
Each branch of this chain has its own unique name, with this flagship outlet in Munich known as "German Schickeria". Occupying a prime position on Gärtnerplatz, it sells a range of women's clothing and accessories.

8. Sendlinger Straße
M4
This traditional shopping street is now home to the modern HOFSTATT – a shopping mall.

9. Servus Heimat
M4 Sendlingerstraße 1
Not your average souvenir shop, this place specializes in fun trinkets for fans of the Bavarian way of life.

10. Stachus-Passagen
M3 Karlsplatz
There are nearly 60 shops and restaurants occupying the lower floor of the S-Bahn.

Pubs, Bars and Clubs

1. Kilians Irish Pub
📍 M3 🏠 Frauenplatz 11 🌐 hilians irishpub.de

Sip on some Guinness while enjoying live music at this popular pub. There is karaoke every Sunday.

2. Niederlassung
📍 F5 🏠 Buttermelcherstraße 6
🕐 Sun & Mon 🌐 niederlassung.org

There's an excellent gin selection (over 60 types) at this pub. Happy hours are from 7 to 9pm and again after midnight.

3. Paradiso Tanzbar
📍 F5 🏠 Rumfordstraße 2 🕐 10pm–5:30am Fri & Sat 🌐 paradiso-tanzbar.de

This club, with crystal chandeliers, red velvet and mirrors, featured in Freddie Mercury's *Living on My Own* video.

4. Zephyr Bar
📍 F5 🏠 Baaderstraße 68
🕐 Mon

One of the many bars in this area, Zephyr is a long-standing favourite among locals.

5. Der Kleine Kranich
📍 F3 🏠 Neureutherstraße 21
🕐 Sun–Tue 🌐 derhkleinehranich.de

This cosy café has a small food menu, great drinks and a terrace outside.

Band performing at the Kilians Irish Pub

6. Buena Vista Bar
📍 N4 🏠 Am Einlass 2a 🕐 Mon
🌐 buena-vista-bar.de

A friendly Cuban bar, Buena Vista serves tasty cocktails and tapas. As the evening progresses, tables are cleared to make way for salsa dancing.

7. Flushing Meadows
📍 F5 🏠 Fraunhoferstraße 32
🌐 flushingmeadowshotel.com

Visit this rooftop bar for great drinks, spectacular views and a relaxed atmosphere.

8. Bohne & Malz
📍 L4 🏠 Sonnenstraße 11
🌐 bohneundmalz.de

Enjoy breakfasts, Mediterranean-style dishes and cocktails at this pub. It has outdoor seating too.

9. Bahnwärter Thiel
📍 E6 🏠 Tumblingerstraße 45 🕐 Hours vary, chech website 🌐 bahnwaerter thiel.de

Set against a backdrop of shipping containers and subway cars, this spot hosts stand-up comedy and DJ sets.

10. Milchbar
📍 M4 🏠 Sonnenstraße 27 🕐 From 10pm Mon–Thu, from 11pm Fri & Sat
🌐 milchundbar.de

Fans of house and electro flock here for the DJ sets. Start the week with the regular Blue Monday 1980s party.

Places to Eat

**Entrance to the famous
Schneider Bräuhaus**

1. Augustiner Stammhaus

🗺 M3 🏠 Neuhauser Straße 27
🌐 augustiner-restaurant.com · €
A local Bavarian favourite, Zum
Augustiner has a mussel hall
and an arcaded garden.

2. Bratwurstherzl

🗺 N4 🏠 Dreifaltigheitsplatz 1
🚫 Sun 🌐 bratwurstherzl.de · €
Bavarian classics such as *Saueres
Kalbslüngerl* (pickled veal's lung)
or *Saure Zipfel* (pickled sausage)
are served here.

3. Nürnberger Bratwurst
Glöckl am Dom

🗺 M3 🏠 Frauenplatz 9
🌐 bratwurst-gloeckl.de · €
Among the dishes on offer here is
the famous *Rostbratwürste mit Kraut*
(barbecued sausages with cabbage).
The menu, which focuses on seasonal
dishes, changes daily.

4. Landersdorfer
and Innerhofer

🗺 M4 🏠 Hachenstraße 6–8
🚫 Sat & Sun 🌐 landersdorferund
innerhofer.de · €€€
This traditional restaurant has
an extensive wine list, set menus
and a convivial atmosphere.

5. Prinz Myshkin

🗺 M4 🏠 Hachenstraße 2 🌐 prinz
myshkin.com · €
Creative vegan and vegetarian cuisine
is served in an elegant setting at
Prinz Myshkin.

6. Schneider Bräuhaus

🗺 N4 🏠 Tal 7 🌐 schneider-brauhaus.
de · €
The flavours of Munich are at their best
here: offal, sausage and roast pork
served with cold Schneider Weisse beer.

7. Café Glockenspiel

🗺 N3 🏠 Marienplatz 28 (entrance on
Rosenstraße) 🌐 cafe-glockenspiel.de
· €
Set in the centre of the city, this cosy
café offers homemade cakes by day
and international cuisine at night.

8. Café Rischart

🗺 N4 🏠 Vihtualienmarkt 2
🌐 rischart.de · €
This café has a terrace with beautiful
views. Its flagship branch can be
found on Marienplatz.

9. Café Frischhut

🗺 N4 🏠 Prälat-Zistl-Straße 8
📞 (089) 268237
The only items on the menu here
are doughnuts and pastries, which
are served with hot drinks.

10. Der Pschorr

🗺 N4 🏠 Vihtualienmarkt 15
📞 (089) 44238 3940 · €€
From its restaurant, beer garden
and terrace, Der Pschorr offers
Bavarian cuisine.

NORTHERN OLD TOWN

Extending north from Marienplatz as far as the top of the Altstadtring, this northern part of the Old Town is a mix of the old and new. The area was once defined by the medieval city wall and the Schwabinger Tor. This gate formed part of the second set of town ramparts, until it was torn down in 1817 to create the junction between Odeonsplatz and Ludwigstraße. The area itself is a treasure trove of historical sights with the Frauenkirche, the Theatinerkirche and the Residenz, and its Hofgarten, all located here. Sat alongside this history are elegant modern shopping streets and a buzzing hub of nightlife around Maximiliansplatz. In spite of these attractions, it is a smaller square that is better known by far: Platzl, home to the world's most famous beer hall, the Hofbräuhaus.

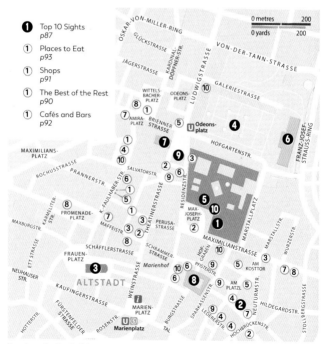

① Top 10 Sights
  p87

① Places to Eat
  p93

① Shops
  p91

① The Best of the Rest
  p90

① Cafés and Bars
  p92

For places to stay in this area, see p146

Patrons at Munich's famous Hofbräuhaus

1 Nationaltheater

N3 Max-Joseph-Platz 2
staatsoper.de

The Nationaltheater has been the home of opera in Munich since it opened in 1818 and became famous for its performances of Wagnerian operas. Indeed, it was here that his famous operas *Tristan und Isolde*, *Die Walküre* and *Rheingold* were first performed. Outside of opera, the theatre is also home to the state orchestra and ballet, with many performances held here. The annual Opernfestspiele *(see p74)* brings fans here from around the world. It offers behind-the-scenes tours everyday.

2 Platzl and Hofbräuhaus

N3 Am Platzl 9
hofbraeuhaus.de

Munich and beer go back a long way: the Hofbräuhaus (1897) originated from a brewery (Hofbräu) founded by Wilhelm V in 1589. To this day, Hofbräu remains a Bavarian brand. The pub offers space for a thousand drinkers in its ground-floor bar, while the first floor is home to a ceremonial hall with a barrel vault ceiling, as well as a quieter bar. Outside the building itself, the Hofbräuhaus has an attractive beer garden sheltered by chestnut trees. It goes without saying that Hofbräu is served on tap – around 10,000 litres (17,600 pints) a day, in fact. Away from the beer hall, the winding side streets that run off Platzl are the oldest part of Munich.

3 Frauenkirche

Visible from much of the city centre, the Frauenkirche's twin towers dominate the Munich skyline. The design for this enormous church *(p24)* originally included Gothic spires, but unfortunately there was not enough money left to build them. It was not until 36 years later that the Frauenkirche's domes were added, and these would effectively become the model for all subsequent Bavarian onion domes.

Onion domes atop the towers of the Frauenkirche

4 Hofgarten

🔲 N2–3

Head through the Hofgarten archway on Odeonsplatz to reach this Renaissance garden, which was established while the Residenz was undergoing its extension work. It is one of the largest Mannerist gardens north of the Alps.

5 Residenz

Munich's must-see palace *(p26)* was built over the centuries as a city-centre residence for the Wittelsbach rulers of Bavaria, after they outgrew the Alter Hof. A must for architecture enthusiasts, the palace features a lavish Renaissance Hall of Antiquities, rich Rococo decorations in the Ancestral Gallery and striking Neo-Classical flourishes in the Charlotte rooms.

6 Staatskanzlei

🔲 N2–3 🔲 Franz-Josef-Strauß-Ring 1 🔲

The Bayerische Staatskanzlei (Bavarian State Chancellery; 1993), behind the Hofgarten, was the source of much controversy due to its ultra-modern design. Today, the complex combines the renovated cupola of the former army museum and a modern glass construction. The building is not open to the public, but visitors can still view its impressive exterior.

7 Theatinerkirche

🔲 N3 🔲 Theatinerstraße 22
🔲 Church: 7am–9pm daily; crypt: May–Oct: 11:30am–3pm Mon–Sat
🔲 theatinerkirche.de

The construction of the St Catejan court church, also known as the Theatinerkirche, was begun in 1663 by Agostino Barelli. Enrico Zuccalli took over the project in 1674, and it was 100 years before François de Cuvilliés designed the Rococo façade. The crypt is the final resting place of the Wittelsbachs.

8 Alter Hof

🔲 N3 🔲 Burgstraße 4
🔲 10am–6pm Mon–Sat

Set to the northeast of Marienhof (behind the Neues Rathaus), the Alter Hof is best reached via an archway among the old townhouses on Burgstraße. The first Residenz of the Wittelsbachs within the city walls was built between 1253 and 1255. Original features include the west wing, which has its own gatehouse adorned with coats of arms, and a tower-like bay window known as the Affenturm (Monkey's Tower). Legend has it that the court monkey kidnapped Ludwig IV (who would later become emperor of Germany), and climbed with him to the top of the turret. Fortunately, the monkey brought the boy back safe and sound. The vaulted cellar of the Alter Hof contains a permanent exhibition on Bavarian castles, which includes information on the former Residenz.

Arches of the Italianate-styled Feldherrnhalle

A DAY IN THE NORTHERN OLD TOWN

Morning

Start at the **Frauenkirche** (p24). After exploring the cathedral, go around the building to Albertgasse. At the end of the alley is Marienhof; cross to get to **Dallmayr** (p91). After visiting the delicatessen, head to the Alter Hof. Take a left here onto Sparkassenstraße and just a few steps left again will get you to **Hofbräuhaus at Platzl** (p93). Head north past Platzl to **Maximilianstraße** (p91). After taking in the smart shops and boutiques on the way, you will pass the **Staatsoper** before arriving back at Theatinerstraße. A great place to stop for coffee and a quick snack is **Aran Fünf Höfe** (Theatinerstraße 12).

Afternoon

Once you've enjoyed a pit stop, explore the **Fünf Höfe** (p91), or the Kunsthalle. Next, head to the **Salvatorkirche** (p90) and **Literaturhaus** (p90). Salvatorstraße will take you back to Theatinerstraße again. Keep left for **Odeonsplatz** (p22), where you will find the **Theatinerkirche** and **Feldherrnhalle**. Depending on the weather, you can spend the afternoon outside in the **Hofgarten** or at the **Residenz** (p26). Once you've worked up an appetite, the **Spatenhaus an der Oper** (p70) is the perfect place to round off the day in style.

9 Feldherrnhalle
N3 Odeonsplatz

Ludwig I commissioned Friedrich von Gärtner to build the Feldherrnhalle on the site of the Schwabinger Tor, a medieval watchtower, based on the Loggia dei Lanzi in Florence. The building was completed in 1844 and blends perfectly with the old and new towns between which it stands. The aim had been to create a focal point that would close off Ludwigstraße and give the irregular Odeonsplatz a more ordered appearance. The statues here represent the Bavarian Feldherren (generals), the Count von Tilly and Baron von Wrede. The entrance steps are guarded by two lions. The building is not open to the public and can only be viewed from the outside.

10 Residenztheater
N3 Max-Joseph-Platz 1
residenztheater.de

After the destruction of the Residenztheater in World War II, a new building was constructed between the Residenz and Nationaltheater. It is home to the magnificent Bavarian State Theatre, which sets the standard for German-language productions. Visitors are welcomed by a beautiful light installation, created by artist Ingo Maurer.

Famous Monkey Tower at Alter Hof

The Best of the Rest

1. Wittelsbacherplatz
Ⓟ N2

Wittelsbacherplatz, the square just to the west of Odeonsplatz, is home to Ludwig Ferdinand's palace (now the headquarters of Siemens) and an equestrian statue of Maximilian I.

2. Max-Joseph-Platz
Ⓟ N3

The Maximilian I Joseph memorial can be found in this early 19th-century square, which began with the construction of the Nationaltheater opera house. In summer, "Oper für alle" (Opera for all) streams the live performance on a giant screen.

Intricate rib vaulting at Salvatorkirche

3. Kunsthalle
Ⓟ N3   **Ⓛ** Theatinerstraße 8   **Ⓞ** 10am–8pm daily   **Ⓦ** kunsthalle-muc.de

Built in 2001, the Kunsthalle, nestled in the glitzy Fünf Höfe shopping centre, hosts three to four high-profile exhibitions each year.

4. Literaturhaus
Ⓟ N3   **Ⓛ** Salvatorplatz 1   **Ⓦ** literaturhaus-muenchen.de

Located in a former Renaissance school, the Literaturhaus is used for literary gatherings and exhibitions. Brasserie OskarMaria (p92) is on the ground floor.

5. Palais Porcia
Ⓟ N3   **Ⓛ** Kardinal-Faulhaber-Straße 12

The Rococo façade of this 1693 palace was designed by François de Cuvilliés the Elder.

6. Promenadeplatz
Ⓟ M3

In medieval times, this long, narrow square with its five memorials functioned as a salt market. The famous Hotel Bayerischer Hof and the Palais Montgelas now occupy its northern side.

7. Münchner Kammerspiele
Ⓟ N3   **Ⓛ** Maximilianstraße 28   **Ⓦ** muenchner-kammerspiele.de

An Art Nouveau masterpiece, this theatre hosts plays, music and dance.

8. Erzbischöfliches Palais
Ⓟ N3   **Ⓛ** Kardinal-Faulhaber-Straße 7

Formally the Palais Holnstein, the official residence of the archbishop is yet another creation of Cuvilliés the Elder, dating from 1737.

9. Alte Münze
Ⓟ N3   **Ⓛ** Hofgraben 4

The Münzhof (mint), dating from 1567, has a three-storey arcaded courtyard that was once home to stables, a library and an art chamber belonging to Albrecht V. The official state mint was established here in the 19th century.

10. Salvatorkirche
Ⓟ N3   **Ⓛ** Salvatorstraße 17

Originally built in 1493–4, the Gothic cemetery church for the Frauenkirche has been a Greek Orthodox place of worship since 1829.

Shops and Shopping Areas

1. Fünf Höfe
📍 N3 Theatinerstraße 15
🌐 fuenfhoefe.de
Brimming with restaurants and shops, this shopping centre is a local favourite and attracts millions of visitors every year.

2. Theatinerstraße and Residenzstraße
📍 N3
The shops on these streets appeal to fashionistas with refined tastes.

3. Maximilianstraße
📍 N3
Munich's most expensive shopping street, Maximilianstraße features various international luxury labels.

4. OBACHT'
📍 N4 Ledererstraße 17
This shop on the corner of the Hofbräuhaus sells trinkets and curios with a local touch – perfect for souvenirs to take home.

5. Nymphenburger Porzellan
📍 N2 Odeonsplatz 1
The flagship store of the Porzellan Manufaktur Nymphenburg, located in the Nymphenburg rotunda, is popular with lovers of design and porcelain alike.

6. Manufactum
📍 N3 Dienerstraße 12
A fitting venue for this warehouse of self-proclaimed "good things", Manufactum is located in the grounds of the Alter Hof, the first Residenz.

7. Lodenfrey
📍 N3 Maffeistraße 5–7
While the traditional *Dirndl* and *Lederhosen* can be found in many places in Munich, the costumes here are of the highest quality.

8. Elly Seidl
📍 N3 Maffeistraße 1
Locals can't get enough of the handmade pralines sold by this family-run company.

9. Team shops: FC Bayern and TSV 1860 München
📍 N3 Orlandostraße 1 and 8
Football kits and all kinds of team memorabilia can be found in these two shops, close to the Hofbräuhaus.

10. Dallmayr
📍 N3 Dienerstraße 14
The Marienhof branch of the former purveyor to the court has a top delicatessen and its own coffee blends. Its restaurant has two Michelin stars, and there's a lovely café bistro, too.

Shoppers at the Fünf Höfe shopping centre

Outdoor seating at Café Luitpold

Cafés and Bars

1. Brasserie OskarMaria
Q N3 **A** Salvatorplatz 1 **W** oskar maria.com
OskarMaria's brasserie in the Literaturhaus serves its dishes on designer tableware (with quotes by Oskar Maria Graf). The outdoor seating is available in summer.

2. Café Kreutzkamm
Q N3 **A** Maffeistraße 4 **W** kreutz kamm.de
The home of the finest pralines and biscuits, this traditional café is the perfect spot in which to indulge.

3. Schumann's Tagesbar
Q N3 **A** Maffeistraße 6 **C** Sun **W** schumanns.de
This Fünf Höfe branch of the legendary Schumann's is a popular meeting place. Open during the day only.

4. Bar Centrale
Q N4 **A** Ledererstraße 23 **W** bar-centrale.com
A stylish Italian retro bar, Centrale serves espressos in the morning and cocktails after sundown.

5. Pusser's
Q N3 **A** Falkenturmstraße 9
Pusser's is a classic piano bar with a menu of over 200 cocktails.

6. Tambosi
Q N2 **A** Odeonsplatz 18 **W** tambosi-odeonsplatz.de
One of the oldest cafés in the city, Tambosi is a good place to enjoy a cup of coffee.

7. Café Luitpold
Q N2 **A** Brienner Straße 11 **W** cafe-luitpold.de
Serving homemade pralines, cakes and daily specials, this former coffee house was rebuilt with its own palm garden after the war. It has a beautiful inner courtyard and a fabulous conservatory.

8. Alvino Bar
Q N2 **A** Brienner Straße 10 **C** Sun **W** baralvino.de
Located near the Hofgarten, this fun spot is one of the city's best bars.

9. Café Maelu
Q N3 **A** Theatinerstraße 32 **W** maelu.de
From macarons to tarts, this coffee shop in the Theatiner arcade offers a selection of mouth-watering confections.

10. Schumann's
Q N2 **A** Odeonsplatz 6–7 **W** schumanns.de
Among the best places in the city for a drink, this Munich institution has been in operation since 1982.

Restaurants

1. Pageou
N3 Kardinal-Faulhaber-Straße 10 Sun & Mon pageou.de · €€€
The home of chef Ali Güngörmüş and his Middle Eastern cuisine.

2. Buffet Kull
N4 Marienstraße 4 Mon buffet-kull.de · €€
Innovative Mediterranean cuisine is on the menu at this restaurant.

3. Pfälzer Residenz Weinstube
N3 Residenzstraße 1 pfaelzerweinstube.de · €
The Residenz, with six lounges, a wine cellar and outdoor seating, serves specialities such as *Saumagen* (sow's stomach), plus the best wines from the Palatinate region.

4. Hofbräuhaus
N3 Am Platzl 9 hofbraeuhaus.de · €
Well known for its *Schweinshaxe* (ham hock) dishes, the Hofbräuhaus also has good vegetarian options.

5. Südtiroler Stuben
N3 Am Platzl 8 Sun schuhbeck.de · €€€
Enjoy gourmet fare at this restaurant situated on the Platzl.

6. Restaurant Alois
N3 Dienerstraße 14–15 Sun–Tue dallmayr.com · €€€
Chef Rosina Ostler serves spectacular six- and eight-course menus at this Michelin-starred restaurant on the first floor of the traditional delicatessen Dallmayr.

7. Matsuhisa Munich
N3 Neuturmstraße 1 mandarinoriental.com · €€€
The only restaurant in Germany headed by top chef Nobu Matsuhisa serves exquisite Japanese fusion cuisine.

8. Kulisse Theater-Restaurant
N3 Maximilianstraße 26 (089) 294728 Sun · €€
For over 50 years, the Kulisse restaurant, housed in the Kammerspiele theatre, has been serving fresh seasonal fare in a sophisticated atmosphere.

9. Restaurant Pfistermühle
N3 Pfisterstraße 4 Mon & Sun pfistermuehle.de · €€€
The vault of this 16th-century former ducal mill offers the finest in Bavarian cuisine. Lunchtime express menu available for €20.

10. Azuki
N3 Hofgraben 9/Ecke Maximilianstraße azukimunich.com · €€
Located in a former post office with beautiful arcades, this restaurant serves Japanese and Vietnamese cuisine.

Beef tenderloin with fries at Buffet Kull

MUSEUM QUARTER

The museum quarter (officially known as "Kunstareal München") is located in the Maxvorstadt district, bordering the university quarter. This is where you will find many of Bavaria's best museums, along with the top art museums – the three Pinakotheken, Museum Brandhorst and the Egyptian Art Museum – among other world-class attractions. Nearby are further art and scuplture museums, including the Glyptothek, Antikensammlungen and Lenbachhaus, along with various smaller collections and a number of scientific museums, including the Paläontologisches Museum. With a wide selection of private galleries to boot, this is an area where culture and art lovers can easily spend a couple of days or more. There are plenty of cafés and bars where you can take a break in between museum visits. Alternatively, pack a picnic to enjoy in the parkland around the Pinakotheken.

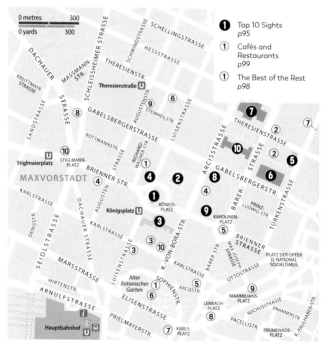

1 Top 10 Sights
p95

1 Cafés and Restaurants
p99

1 The Best of the Rest
p98

For places to stay in this area, see p147

1 Königsplatz

L2

The city has Ludwig I to thank for this spacious square, with architect Leo von Klenze behind the Doric Propylaea and Ionian Glyptothek, which were built between 1816 and 1862. During the Nazi era, the square was paved and served as a parade ground. These days it is a green space and hosts outdoor events in the summer.

2 Glyptothek

M2 Königsplatz 3 10am–5pm Tue–Sun (to 8pm Thu) antike-am-koenigsplatz.mwn.de

Munich's oldest public museum, the Glyptothek is housed in a resplendent building, reminiscent of a Greek temple. It is regarded as architect Leo von Klenze's finest Neo-Classical work. Highlights include 2,500-year-old archaic figures, the bust of Roman Emperor Augustus and the spectacularly lascivious Barberini Faun. The café is located in Room VIII and also offers seating out in the tranquil courtyard.

3 Staatliche Antikensammlungen

L2 Königsplatz 1 10am–5pm Tue–Sun (to 8pm Wed) antike-am-koenigsplatz.mwn.de

This collection of antiquities includes Greek, Etruscan and Roman vases,

Dionysus cup,
Staatliche
Antikensammlungen

and bronze, terracotta, glass and jewellery from the 3rd millennium BCE to the 5th century CE.

4 Städtische Galerie im Lenbachhaus

L2 Luisenstraße 33 10am–6pm Tue–Sun (to 8pm Thu) lenbachhaus.de

Franz von Lenbach's villa (1887–91) has its own living quarters, studio wing, a further wing extension and a historic garden. A shining brass cube was added during extensive renovations completed in 2013. Thanks to a world-first combination of daylight and LEDs, the famous Blue Rider collection and other works can be seen in a new light. Both the exhibition space on the U-Bahn mezzanine and Café Ella belong to the museum.

Grand villa and gardens, Städtische Galerie im Lenbachhaus

Modern façade of the Museum Brandhorst

5 Museum Brandhorst

🚇 M2 🏛 Theresienstraße 35a
🕐 10am–6pm Tue–Sun (until 8pm Thu) 🌐 museum-brandhorst.de 🔗

Opened in 2009, this museum occupies a purpose-built multicoloured building by Berlin-based architects Sauerbruch Hutton. The polygonal area above the foyer was designed specially for Cy Twombly's famous *Lepanto* cycle. Dominating some of the space are more of Twombly's large canvasses, while Andy Warhol is represented by some of his Elvis works, among others. Gerhard Richter's work makes an appearance, as do artists including Jeff Koons, Sigmar Polke, Alex Katz and Mike Kelley. The Horst Esskultur-Bar is situated in the foyer.

6 Pinakothek der Moderne

This enormous building (p30) was designed by Stephan Braunfels as a temple to 20th- and 21st-century art and design. All of its rooms are grouped around a central rotunda. The café offers indoor and outdoor seating.

7 Neue Pinakothek

One of the three museums that form the Pinakotheken (p28), the Neue Pinakothek opened in 1981. It was constructed on the same site as its predecessor, which had been destroyed in World War II. Based on plans by Alexander von Brancas, the building offers exceptional lighting within its internal spaces, which are packed with world-class artworks. The Hunsinger restaurant here has outdoor tables on the terrace to enjoy the sunny days. The museum is undergoing extensive renovation and will be closed until 2029.

8 Staatliches Museum Ägyptischer Kunst

🚇 M2 🏛 Gabelsbergerstraße 35
🕐 10am–8pm Tue, 10am–6pm Wed–Sun 🌐 smaeh.de 🔗

The entrance to this museum on the site of the University of Television and Film Munich (HFF) is reminiscent of the entrance to a burial chamber in the Valley of the Kings, leading into underground halls around a sunken courtyard. The ramp to the exhibition space leads to a superb statue of the god Horus. Further highlights include a facial fragment of Akhenaten, the coffin mask of Queen Sitdjehutj, and a statue of High Priest Bakenkhonsu.

9 NS-Dokumentations-zentrum

🚇 M2 🏛 Brienner Straße 34 🕐 10am–7pm Tue–Sun 🌐 nsdoku.de 🔗

A place of education and remembrance, this documentation centre presents

Munich's past as the "Capital of the Movement". Opened in 2015, this cuboid structure of exposed white concrete stands on a historic spot: it was once the site of the "Brown House", the national headquarters of the Nazi Party. The permanent exhibition, "München und der Nationalsozialismus" (Munich and National Socialism), includes photographs, documents, texts, film projections and media stations.

10 Alte Pinakothek

This elongated building (p28) designed by Leo von Klenze has spacious rooms illuminated by skylights along with smaller cabinets on its north side, making it a model for other museum buildings of the early 19th century. The Alte Pinakothek suffered heavy damage in World War II, but it had been successfully rebuilt by 1957, with missing parts of the façade replaced by new, unrendered brickwork rather than reconstructed. The green spaces feature a sculpture exhibition, while the English-themed Café Klenze pays homage to the building's architects and is a good place for a break between museums.

Browsing artworks at the Alte Pinakothek

EXPLORING THE MUSEUM QUARTER

Morning

A good breakfast at **Café Lotti** (p99) on Schleißheimer Straße will set you up for the museum tour. Head to your first highlight – the **Lenbachhaus** (p95). Here, stop to browse the collections, or move on to the next museum. If you decide to keep going, turn left onto **Königsplatz** (p95), where you'll find the **Glyptothek** (p95) and **Antikensammlungen** (p95). Straight ahead takes you to the **NS-Dokumentationszentrum**. Next, visit the **Alte Pinakothek** and **Pinakothek der Moderne**. Make your way across the lawn in front of Pinakothek der Moderne and take in the colourful façade of **Museum Brandhorst**. Then, head around the museum building and treat yourself to an ice cream from **Ballabeni** (Theresienstraße 46). For something more substantial, keep going until you reach **Tresznjewski** (p99).

Afternoon

Follow Theresienstraße, then turn left onto Barer Straße to reach the **Alte Pinakothek**. If you're interested in ancient Egypt, then take a left onto Arcisstraße and walk down to the **Staatliches Museum Ägyptischer Kunst**. From here, follow Arcisstraße across Katharina-von-Bora-Straße and see the day out at **Park Café** (p99).

The Best of the Rest

Bronze obelisk in the centre of Karolinenplatz

1. Paläontologisches Museum
📍 L2 🏛 Richard-Wagner-Straße 10
🕐 8am–4pm Mon–Thu, 8am–2pm Fri
🌐 palmuc.org

Expect to find prehistoric fossils of dinosaurs, mammoths, sabre-toothed tigers and the Mühldorf prehistoric elephant here.

2. Museum Mineralogia
📍 N2 🏛 Theresienstraße 41
🕐 1–5pm Tue–Sun 🌐 msm.snsb.de 🔗

This museum holds a collection of minerals, crystals, precious stones, meteorites and much more.

3. Basilika St Bonifaz
📍 L2 🏛 Karlstraße 34

Dating back to 1850, this abbey is the final resting place of Ludwig I.

4. Hochschule für Musik und Theater
📍 M2 🏛 Arcisstraße 12

In the former "Führerbau" (Führer's building), this university is Germany's oldest training centre for theatre and music students. It also holds concerts.

5. Karolinenplatz
📍 M2

A black obelisk to commemorate those who fell in Napoleon's Russian Campaign of 1812 stands in this square, along with Amerikahaus and the stock exchange.

6. Alter Botanischer Garten
📍 L3 🏛 Sophienstraße 7

This former botanical garden is now a park, home to the Neptune fountain.

7. Justizpalast
📍 L3 🏛 Prielmayerstraße 7

Built by Friedrich Thiersch in 1890–97, the Palace of Justice and its atrium dominate Karlsplatz/Stachus.

8. Lenbachplatz
📍 M3

This green square is always buzzing with activity, and includes the Neo-Classical Wittelsbacherbrunnen fountain.

9. Maximiliansplatz
📍 M3

Some of Munich's most popular clubs are situated around this park-style square with its many memorials.

10. Löwenbräukeller
📍 E4 🏛 Stiglmaierplatz
🌐 loewenbraeukeller.com

This 19th-century building has several rooms, a ceremonial hall and a large beer garden.

Gomphotherium skeleton at the Paläontologisches Museum

Cafés and Restaurants

1. Park Café
📍 L3 🏛 Sophienstraße 7
🌐 parkhcafe089.de · €€
This café occupies the site of the 1854 Glaspalast exhibition hall before it burned down. Great beer garden.

2. Tresznjewski
📍 F4 🏛 Theresienstraße 72
🌐 tresznjewski.com · €
Breakfast, lunch and dinner are served both inside and out at this café. In the evenings it transforms into a cocktail bar.

3. Hans im Glück
📍 L2 🏛 Luisenstraße 14
🌐 hansimgluech-burgergrill.de · €
This burger paradise has something for every-one from beef lovers to vegans, and is great for satisfying post-pub hunger cravings.

4. Hamburgerei
📍 L2 🏛 Brienner Straße 49
🌐 hamburgerei.de · €
The burgers at this joint are made with only the freshest ingredients. Crunchy salads and vegetarian and vegan options are also on offer.

5. Hoiz
📍 M2 🏛 Karlstraße 10 🗓 Sun
🌐 hoiz.restaurant · €€
This cosy brasserie offers a small selection of high-quality dishes at reasonable prices.

6. Nasca
📍 E3 🏛 Enhuberstrasse 1 🗓 Sun & Mon 🌐 nascarestaurantcom.wpcomstaging.com · €€
Nasca is a taste of Peru in the heart of Munich, with many national delicacies.

7. Katzentempel München
📍 F4 🏛 Türkenstraße 29
🌐 katzentempel.de · €€
A modern interior, a menu of vegan food and several resident cats are

PRICE CATEGORIES

Price of a three-course meal (or similar) for one, with a glass of wine or beer, including taxes and service.

€ below €30 €€ €30–60 €€€ over €60

Outdoor seating at the popular Tresznjewski

the main attractions at this friendly lunch spot near the Brandhorst.

8. Café Lotti
📍 E3 🏛 Schleißheimer Straße 13
🌐 cafe-lotti.cafe · €
This pink, parlour-style café serves breakfast and light bites.

9. Café Jasmin
📍 E3 🏛 Steinheilstraße 20
🌐 cafe-jasmin.com · €
Furniture from the 1950s and panoramic wallpaper set the scene for a hearty (often organic) meal.

10. Baalbek
📍 L2 🏛 Karlstraße 27 🗓 Sun
🌐 restaurant-baalbeh.de · €€€
Homemade-style Lebanese food is the speciality of this popular restaurant. It also has outdoor seating on the terrace.

SCHWABING AND THE UNIVERSITY QUARTER

Schwabing was a separate village in its own right until it was incorporated into Munich in 1890. It became a well-known alternative district, inhabited by artists and intellectuals. Its characteristic boulevard, Leopoldstraße, which becomes Ludwigstraße, is lined with elegant Neo-Classical buildings, most of them government offices and public buildings, including the Bavarian State Library and the university.

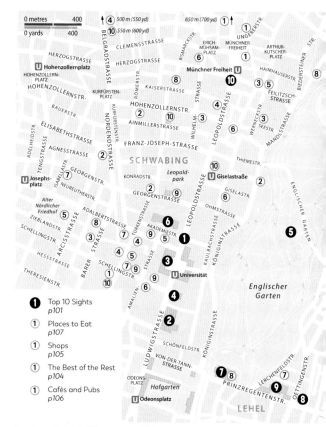

1	Top 10 Sights	p101
1	Places to Eat	p107
1	Shops	p105
1	The Best of the Rest	p104
1	Cafés and Pubs	p106

For places to stay in this area, see p147

Munich's monumental Siegestor

1 Ludwigstraße and Siegestor

Q F3

Ludwig I commissioned a monumental boulevard in Italian Renaissance style. This "Italian mile" is bounded by the Feldherrnhalle (*p89*) to the south and the Siegestor to the north. Modelled on the Arch of Constantine in Rome, the Siegestor is crowned by the figure of Bavaria riding a chariot drawn by four lions. Designed for victory parades honouring the Bavarian army, the gate was inscribed after the war with lines that translate as "Dedicated to victory, destroyed in war, an entreaty for peace".

2 Bayerische Staatsbibliothek

Q N2   **Q** Ludwigstraße 16
W bsb-muenchen.de

This 16th-century research library holds over 10 million books and 130,000 manuscripts, and features the collections of Albrecht V and Wilhelm V. The present building was built by Friedrich von Gärtner in the style of a Renaissance palace.

3 Ludwig-Maximilians-Universität

Q F3   **Q** Geschwister-Scholl-Platz
W uni-muenchen.de

In 1826 Ludwig I moved the university founded in 1472 in Ingolstadt to Munich. Its main assembly hall looks out onto Geschwister-Scholl-Platz and is surrounded by faculty buildings.

4 Ludwigskirche

Q F4   **Q** Ludwigstraße 20

This Italian Romanesque-style university church was built between 1829 and 1843. King Ludwig I commissioned Friedrich von Gärtner to build the church that bears the monarch's name, on his new boulevard, Ludwigstraße. The church's façade, with its triple-arched entrance, is watched over by figures of Christ and the four Evangelists. *The Last Judgment* altar fresco by Peter Cornelius is the second-largest altar fresco in the world.

Magnificent frescoes adorning Ludwigskirche

5 Englischer Garten and Chinesischer Turm

Schwabing's "back garden" is a recreational paradise *(p32)*. The side streets to the right of Ludwigstraße and Leopoldstraße lead to two popular beer gardens: the Chinesischer Turm *(chinaturm.de)* and Seehaus on Kleinhesseloher See.

6 Akademie der Bildenden Künste

🇩 F3 🇩 Akademiestraße 2–4 🇩 adbk.de

The Academy of Fine Arts, set in a Neo-Renaissance style building constructed between 1808 and 1886, has had an eventful history. The list of students who attended around 1900 reads like a who's who of modern art, including Kandinsky and Klee. An exhibition gallery is located on site.

7 Haus der Kunst

🇩 P2 🇩 Prinzregentenstraße 1 🇩 10am–8pm Wed–Mon (to 10pm Thu) 🇩 hausderkunst.de 🇩

The Nazi past of the "House of German Art", dating from 1937, is documented in a free exhibition in the entrance area. The Haus der Kunst is a non-collecting art museum that presents around eight international contemporary art exhibitions every year.

8 Sammlung Schack

🇩 Q3 🇩 Prinzregentenstraße 9 🇩 10am–6pm Wed–Sun 🇩

This collection features around 180 masterpieces of 19th-century German art, mostly landscapes and historical scenes, plus legends and mythology.

9 Bayerisches Nationalmuseum

🇩 P2 🇩 Prinzregentenstraße 3 🇩 10am–5pm Tue–Sun (to 8pm Thu) 🇩 bayerisches-national museum.de 🇩

Packed with exhibits spanning two millennia, this museum offers a journey through the history of

JUGENDSTIL

Munich is the birthplace of Jugendstil, the German version of Art Nouveau. In 1896, the first issue of the art journal *Jugend* (Youth) was published here, giving the new movement – characterized by its decorative, floral and linear style – its name. As early as 1892, over 100 artists had joined forces against the "tyranny" of Franz von Lenbach *(p95)* to form the Munich Secession.

**Meissen porcelain vessel,
Bayerisches Nationalmuseum**

European art and culture. The
building, dating from 1855, is almost
as impressive as the exhibits, and
worth the price of admission alone.

10 Leopoldstraße and Münchner Freiheit

🅰 G1–3

Passing beneath the Siegestor, you
enter Schwabing and the district's
principal promenade: Leopoldstraße,
which is flanked by shops, street-side
cafés and fast-food outlets. One of
the street's highlights is the *Walking
Man* (1995), a 17-m (55-ft) high sculpture by the American artist Jonathan
Borofsky in front of house No 36. At
the northern end of Münchner Freiheit,
in a café of the same name, tables are
set out in summer beneath a larger-
than-life statue of actor Helmut
Fischer, star of German TV series
Monaco Franze – Der ewige Stenz
("The Eternal Dandy"). Art Nouveau
houses can be found on side streets
off Leopoldstraße, notably Georgenstraße (No 8–10) and Ainmiller-straße
(No 20, 22, 33, 34, 35 and 37). Take a
detour onto Kaiserstraße for a glimpse
of a pretty ensemble from the mid-
19th century (Gründerzeit), or head
to Hohenzollernstraße for a host of
boutiques and shops. The other
end of Leopoldstraße leads to
the Englischer Garten.

**Neo-Classical colonnaded
Haus der Kunst**

A DAY IN THE UNIVERSITY QUARTER

Morning

Begin your day at the **Café
Münchner Freiheit** (p106). Later,
stroll down Leopoldstraße and
turn onto Kaiserstraße with its
pretty houses (Lenin once lived
at No 46). Once you reach
Kaiserplatz (p104), head to
Ainmillerstraße with its Jugendstil
houses (nos 20–37). At No 8 (on
Georgenstraße) is the **Pacelli
Palais** (p104). From here, return to
Leopoldstraße and the **Akademie
der Bildenden Künste** near the
Siegestor (p101). Walk to the
University and cross its inner
courtyard, which leads to
the student district around
Amalienstraße, with its many
cafés and restaurants. If you're
ready for a break, visit
Gartensalon (p106) for lunch.

Afternoon

After taking a break, head to the
Englischer Garten. Amble along to
the lovely **Kleinhesseloher See**
(p32) and take in the atmosphere.
Head towards the beer garden at
the **Chinesischer Turm** before
climbing up to **Monopteros** (p32)
to enjoy the city views. Next up, it's
time to check out the **Eisbach
surfers** (p33) and then explore an
exhibition at the **Haus der Kunst**.
See out the evening in style with a
cocktail at **Die Goldene Bar** (p106)
to the northeast.

Cyclists in the tranquil Luitpoldpark

The Best of the Rest

1. Erlöserkirche
G2 **Germaniastraße 4**
This Protestant Art Nouveau church (1899–1901) occupies the northern end of Münchner Freiheit.

2. Elisabethplatz
F3
A piece of old Schwabing, this square is named after the Austrian empress Sisi (short for Elisabeth). A market, open from Monday to Saturday, has been held here since 1903.

3. Wedekindplatz
G2
Renovated in 2014, this square was once the heart of rural Schwabing. In 1962, it was the site of the local riots that have come to be known as the "Schwabinger Krawalle".

4. Luitpoldpark
F1
This park was created out of rubble from World War II. The restaurant in Bamberger House features ornate guest rooms and a beautiful terrace.

5. Alter Nordfriedhof
F3 **Between Zieblandstraße, Arcisstraße, Adalbertstraße & Luisenstraße**
There's nothing morbid about this former cemetery dating back to 1866. It is now a place of recreation and relaxation, and children love to play hide and seek among the old tombstones.

6. Nikolaiplatz & Seidlvilla
G3 **seidlvilla.de**
The Seidlvilla on Nikolaiplatz was saved from demolition and is now a centre for culture and community.

7. Archäologische Staatssammlung
P2 **Lerchenfeldstraße 2**
A collection of ancient and prehistoric discoveries from Bavaria.

8. Kaiserplatz and Kaiserstraße
F2
The silhouette of St Ursula's church on Kaiserplatz has been immortalised by Kandinsky. Kaiserstraße is flanked with ornate buildings from the Gründerzeit.

9. Palais Pacelli
F3 **Georgenstraße 8**
This listed palace is a Neo-Baroque residential building.

10. Walking Man
F3 **Leopoldstraße 36**
Jonathan Borofsky's dynamic 17 m (56 ft) sculpture was commissioned by the Munich Re insurance group.

Shops

1. Breitengrad
F3 · Schellingstraße 29
This shop offers cups and mugs, jewellery, a limited selection of clothing, and bags, not to mention various interesting goodies, such as gold sparklers.

2. Living Colour
F2 · Hohenzollernstraße 39
Clothes, pretty bags, cups, mugs, make-up bags and more – all featuring pretty, vibrant designs.

3. Apartment
F3 · Barer Straße 49
This is another of Munich's shop offering all kinds of colourful products, including tableware, gifts and countless whimsical bits and pieces for kids of all ages.

4. Lehmkuhl
G2 · Leopoldstraße 45
This fine bookshop on Leopoldstraße was founded in 1903 before being taken over by Fritz Lehmkuhl in 1913. It has a distinguished inventory and holds regular author readings.

5. Amsel
F3 · Adalbertstraße 14
amsel-fashion.com
Find traditional Bavarian clothes, such as Dirndls, jackets and vests, made to the highest-possible quality and with serious attention to detail. The store provides great service.

6. Autorenbuchhandlung
F2 · Wilhelmstraße 41
As the name ("Authors' Bookshop") suggests, this bookshop was founded 40 years ago by authors who wanted to free themselves from the book industry. Many author readings are held here.

7. Picknweight
F3 · Schellingstraße 24
Vintage by the kilo: this shop is brimming with second-hand clothes that you pay for by weight. Another branch can be found on Tal.

8. iki M.
F3 · Adalbert Straße 45
A fashion boutique, iki M. features hand-picked vintage pieces. Items are sustainably produced and the set-up is a minimalist's dream.

9. Words' Worth Books
F3 · Schellingstraße 3
wordsworth.de
If you forgot your holiday reading, don't worry. This been-here-forever, English-language bookshop is the place to visit.

10. Dear Goods
F3 · Friedrichstraße 28
This shop stocks only FairTrade, eco-friendly and vegan clothing, shoes and accessories.

Storefront of the trendy Picknweight

Cafés and Pubs

1. Café Münchner Freiheit
⬙ G2 ⬗ Münchner Freiheit 20
This long-established multi-level café with a large outdoor seating area has a larger-than-life sculpture of German actor Helmut Fischer, which overlooks the tables.

2. Café Reitschule
⬙ G3 ⬗ Königinstraße 34
Located at the edge of the Englischer Garten, this traditional café features three patios, a beer garden and a conservatory. From the inside, patrons can see into the riding school. Champagne happy hour runs from 5 to 6:30pm.

3. Cotidiano
⬙ F2 ⬗ Hohenzollernstraße 11
The breakfast menu at this branch of Gärtnerplatz's cult café offers something for everyone, including delicious goods from the in-house bakery. It also serves light bites in the afternoon and evening. Outdoor tables are available.

4. Gartensalon
⬙ F3 ⬗ Türkenstraße 90
⬙ Mon–Fri
Tucked away in an inner courtyard on the Amalienpassage, this café is colourful and kitsch, with rainbow furniture and photo-covered walls. The garden is also a floral paradise. Breakfasts here are particularly good. Cards not accepted.

5. Zeitgeist
⬙ F3 ⬗ Türkenstraße 74
Located close to the University, this well-established café serves amazing breakfasts and coffee.

6. Atzinger
⬙ F3 ⬗ Schellingstraße 9
This once-legendary student pub has been extensively modernized, but the prices remain reasonable.

Alfresco seating at the popular Zeitgeist café

7. Café Ignaz
⬙ F3 ⬗ Georgenstraße 67
This place has been serving delicious organic vegetarian and vegan goodies for over 30 years. It also has its own in-house bakery.

8. Die Goldene Bar
⬙ P2 ⬗ Prinzregentenstraße 1
Located within the Haus der Kunst, this bar takes its name from its golden walls. Enjoy light meals here in the afternoon or stay until evening for cocktails mixed by Klaus St Rainer, former bartender of the year. Outdoor seating is available.

9. Schall & Rauch
⬙ F3 ⬗ Schellingstraße 22
Small, cosy pub, serving local pasta dishes in a friendly atmosphere. Often packed to the rafters.

10. Café Katzentempel
⬙ F4 ⬗ Türkenstraße 29
This vegetarian café is also home to six rescued cats, so you can enjoy a coffee with feline company.

Places to Eat

1. Tantris
G2 ⌂ Johann-Fichte-Straße 7
Noon–4pm & 6:30pm–midnight Wed–Sat ⌨ tantris.de · €€€

This two-Michelin-starred restaurant is Munich's finest for haute cuisine.

2. Georgenhof
F3 ⌂ Friedrichstraße 1
⌨ georgenhof-muenchen.de · €€

An Art Nouveau-style restaurant with beer garden. Be sure to try the pork dishes *Schweinebraten (p66)* or *Schweinshaxe*.

3. Werneckhof Sigi Schelling
G2 ⌂ Werneckstraße 11 Noon–4pm & 6:30pm–midnight Wed–Sat ⌨ werneckhof-schelling.de · €€€

A fine-dining restaurant opened in 2021 with three- to five- course menus. The dress code here is smart casual.

4. Ruff's Burger
F3 ⌂ Türkenstraße 63
⌨ ruffsburger.de · €

Locals love the homemade burgers served here. Ruff's Burger also has six other branches around the city.

5. Occam Deli
G2 ⌂ Feilitzschstraße 15
⌨ occamdeli.com · €

Delicatessen with New York-style snacks and light dishes.

6. Arabesk
P2 ⌂ Kaulbachstraße 86
⌨ arabesh.de · €€

Customers have been enjoying the flavours of the Middle East followed by shisha here for over 30 years. The Lebanese food is delicious.

7. Max-Emanuel-Brauerei
F3 ⌂ Adalbertstraße 33
⌨ max-emanuel.de · €

Dating back to around 1800, this tavern serves traditional Bavarian dishes.

PRICE CATEGORIES

Price of a three-course meal (or similar) for one, with a glass of wine or beer, including taxes and service.

€ below €30 €€ €30–60 €€€ over €60

Its annual white parties to celebrate Carnival, or Fasching, are legendary. Great beer garden with shaded areas.

8. Osterwaldgarten
G2 ⌂ Keferstraße 12 ⌨ schwabinger-osterwaldgarten.de · €€

This beer garden and restaurant at the Englischer Garten serves Bavarian specialities. Make sure to book ahead.

9. Ristorante Pizzeria Bei Mario
F3 ⌂ Adalbertstraße 15 Mon & Tue ⌨ ristorantebeimario.de · €

An Italian restaurant offering Neapolitan pizzas as well as pasta, meat and fish dishes.

10. Restaurant Thu
F2 ⌂ Destouchesstraße 48
Mon ⌨ thu-restaurant.com · €€

Enjoy high-end Vietnamese cuisine at this contemporary restaurant.

The unusually designed ceiling in Tantris

ALONG THE ISAR

Four distinct neighbourhoods flank the right
bank of the Isar river: Giesing, Au, Haidhausen and
Bogenhausen. While Bogenhausen is studded with
villas, Haidhausen is a hotspot for nightlife. To the
west of the Isar, on the left bank, lie the Englischer
Garten and Lehel, a highly sought-after residential
area containing some beautiful historic buildings.
Most of the city's sights and attractions are located
to the east of the river, including the Jugendstil
masterpiece of the Müller'sches Volksbad, the
Maximilianeum and Villa Stuck. Of the two islands
in the middle of the Isar, Museuminsel holds the
Deutsches Museum, a definite highlight in this area.

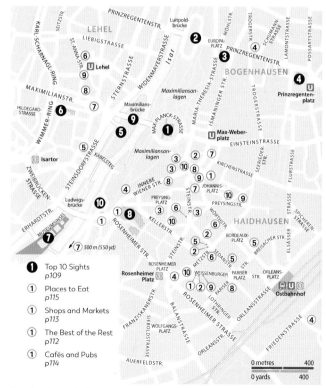

1	Top 10 Sights	*p109*
①	Places to Eat	*p115*
①	Shops and Markets	*p113*
①	The Best of the Rest	*p112*
①	Cafés and Pubs	*p114*

For places to stay in this area, see p148

Stately façade of
the Maximilianeum

1 Maximilianeum

📍 Q4 🏛 Max-Planck-Straße 1
🌐 stiftungmaximilianeum.com

Built by Friedrich Bürklein high
on the banks of the Isar river, the
Maximilianeum was commissioned
by Maximilian II as a school for gifted
students from poor backgrounds.
Though the building has been the
home of the Bavarian parliament
since 1949, a school still occupies its
rear; nowadays it accepts students
with the highest grades.

2 Friedensengel

📍 Q3 🏛 Prinzregentenstraße

Soaring high above the banks of
the Isar, the *Friedensengel* (Angel
of Peace) of 1896–99 commemorates
the Franco–Prussian war of 1870–71.
Based on the Greek goddess Nike, this
gilded figure stands 6 m (19.7 ft) tall.
From its base, two sweeping flights of
stairs lead down an escarpment to
a terraced park with fountains.

*Friedensengel
(Angel of
Peace)*

3 Museum Villa Stuck

📍 G4 🏛 Prinzregentenstraße 60
🕒 For renovation until summer 2025;
chech website 🌐 villastuch.de 🚫

Not far from the Friedensengel is the
Villa Stuck, the *fin-de-siècle* masterpiece of painter Franz von Stuck. A
miller's son, Stuck quickly rose to fame
and was instrumental in the creation
of the Munich Secession in 1892, which
"discovered" Jugendstil (the local version
of Art Nouveau). This villa is now one of
the most important artist residences in
Europe. Stuck combined Neo-Classical,
Art Nouveau and Symbolist elements,
thus underlining his tenet that art
and life were connected. The villa
has served as a museum since 1968
featuring private rooms, a permanent
Art Nouveau collection and changing
exhibitions in the studio wing.

4 Prinzregententheater

📍 H4 🏛 Prinzregentenplatz 12
🌐 theaterahademie.de

This theatre is one of several monumental buildings on this stretch of
Prinzregentenstraße. The Bayerische
Staatstheater perform here, along
with other companies. It was headed
up by August Everding, whose legacy
to the city includes the Bayerische
Theaterakademie, a training ground for
young talent since 1993. Next door is
Prinzregentenbad, a public bath, and
gourmet food shop Feinkost Käfer
(p113), is just across the street.

5 Praterinsel and Alpines Museum

📍 P4 🏠 Praterinsel 5 🕐 10am–6pm Tue–Sun 🌐 alpenverein.de ♿

Located at the southern end of the Praterinsel, an island in the Isar, the Alpines Museum documents the history of mountaineering and features special exhibitions throughout the year. An educational garden showcases the various types of rock found in alpine regions, while exhibitions and events are held in the halls of the former Riemerschmid distillery, located at the northern end of the island. Tango dancers gather in the courtyard on summer evenings.

6 Museum Fünf Kontinente

📍 P3 🏠 Maximilianstraße 42 🕐 9:30am–5:30pm Tue–Sun 🌐 museum-fuenf-kontinente.de ♿

This Neo-Renaissance building dates back to 1859–65 and was originally conceived for the Bayerisches Nationalmuseum. The Ethnological Museum made this its home in 1926 and it features over 160,000 exhibits on the culture of non-European nations, with a collection on Bavarian rulers dating back more than 500 years. The museum café, max2, serves food in the arcades of Maximilanstraße.

Kachina doll, Museum Fünf Kontinente

Health exhibition at the Deutsches Museum

7 Deutsches Museum

Directly southwest from the Müller'sches Volksbad is the Deutsches Museum (p34), the largest museum of science and technology in the world.

8 Gasteig

📍 G5 🏠 Rosenheimer Straße 5 🌐 gasteig.de

The site of the former Bürgerspital hospital and Bürgerbräukeller was transformed into the Gasteig cultural centre between 1978 and 1985, and its tiled bunker design was controversial. It is home to the Munich Philharmonic, the Carl-Orff concert hall and the state library. While the building is being renovated, concerts will take place in the Gasteig HP8 (p73).

9 The Isar Bridges

📍 P3–Q4

The Maximiliansbrücke is actually made up of two distinct bridges: the outer bridge leads to the Maximilianeum, while the inner bridge connects the west bank of the Isar with the Praterinsel. Ludwigsbrücke is another historically important bridge. Henry

HAIDHAUSEN

This area used to lie beyond the city boundaries. A poor, rural village, it was referred to as a Glasscherbenviertel or "broken glass district", and some of the renovated inns are still reminiscent of this period. After 1871, French reparation payments launched development in this area, which explains the French names of the streets here.

the Lion ordered that the original Isarbrücke (built in 1157–8 by the Bishop of Freising) be demolished to make way for a new bridge further to the south, which is where the Ludwigsbrücke is located today. All of the Isar bridges offer lovely views up and down the slow-moving river.

10 Müller'sches Volksbad

🗺 G5 🏠 Rosenheimer Straße 1 ⏰ 7:30am–11pm daily 🌐 swm.de 🅿

Named after Karl Müller, the Munich citizen who financed the project, this Jugendstil bathing temple was built in 1897–1901, based on a design by Carl Hocheder. It was the first public pool in the city and remains one of the most beautiful. It is worth going for a swim just to admire the interior or enjoy the facilities, which include a steam room, though you can visit its stylish café without going for a dip.

The Müller'sches Volksbad next to the Isar

A DAY AROUND THE ISAR

Morning

Setting off from **Müller'sches Volksbad** after coffee or breakfast, turn left out of the baths and along the Isar to the footbridge, which leads to Praterinsel. Walk through the garden of the **Alpines Museum** and across the island to the **Maximilianeum** (p109). Make your way past the building and turn right onto Sckellstraße, which leads to **Wiener Platz** (p112), with its market stalls and the Hofbräukeller. The narrow **An der Kreppe** (p112) lane runs from this square to the historic inns in the "Glasscherbenviertel". The beer garden at the **Hofbräukeller** (p112) is a great place to stop for a break.

Afternoon

After lunch, return to Sckellstraße, cross Max-Planck-Straße and head along Maria-Theresia-Straße, which is flanked by beautiful houses from the Jugendstil period. On the left-hand side of the street, the **Maximiliansanlagen** is a perfect park for a spot of ambling. Regardless of the route you take, all paths will eventually lead you to the **Friedensengel** (p109). Continue along until you reach the Jugendstil **Museum Villa Stuck** (p109). After a tour of the museum, make your way to **Feinkost Käfer** (p113) on Prinzregentenstraße, a treat whether you opt for the deli bistro or the Käfer-Schänke fine-dining restaurant.

The Best of the Rest

Neo-Romanesque interior,
Pfarrkirche St Anna

1. Johanniskirche
⚐ G5 **⌂** Johannisplatz
This Neo-Gothic church has a truly
striking 90-m- (295-ft-) high tower.

2. An der Kreppe
⚐ Q4
Restored inns, originally designed
for brick workers, give this corner of
Haidhausen a village-like character.

3. Wiener Platz and Hofbräukeller
⚐ Q4
At the heart of Haidhausen, Wiener
Platz has hosted a market since 1889,
while the Hofbräukeller *(p61)* has
been here since 1892.

4. Werksviertel
⚐ H6
A former industrial area has been
transformed into a cultural centre
and nightlife hot spot.

5. St Lukas
⚐ P4 **⌂** Mariannenplatz 3
St Luke's, in Lehel, built in 1893–6,
is renowned for its choral concerts.

6. Pfarrkirche St Anna
⚐ P3 **⌂** St-Anna-Platz 5
ⓦ erzbistummuenchen.de
This 19th-century church is the result
of an architecture competition.

7. Maxmonument and Upper Maximilianstraße
⚐ P3
The stretch of Maximilianstraße
from the Altstadtring is flanked by
ornate public buildings. A monument
to Maximilian II (the Maxmonument)
stands at the centre of a roundabout.

8. Regierung von Oberbayern
⚐ P3 **⌂** Maximilianstraße 39
Maximilian II commissioned this Neo-
Gothic building. Today, it serves as the
seat of government for Upper Bavaria.

9. Lehel
⚐ P3–4
Lehel is widely considered to be one
of the city's most beautiful districts.
A stroll in the area, especially in the
vicinity of the Maxmonument, takes
you past some stunning architecture.

10. Weißenburger Platz
⚐ G6
With the Glaspalastbrunnen, a tiered
fountain at its centre, this square
is the hub of the French quarter.
An atmospheric Christmas market
is held here every December.

Towers of St Lukas as seen
from a footbridge

Vintage homeware at Livingroom

Shops and Markets

1. Ypnotic
🗺 G6 📍 Weißenburger Straße 12
Established more than 30 years ago, this independent shop stocks brightly coloured accessories and clothing with unusual designs. Designer labels such as Daily's, Freequent, Malvin and Anonyme can be found here.

2. Weltladen München
🗺 G6 📍 Weißenburger Straße 18
From organic coffee to handmade paper from India, this shop sells all sorts of fair trade products from around the world.

3. Livingroom
🗺 Q4 📍 Wiener Platz 2
This shop stocks vintage furniture and accessories for the kitchen, bathroom and living room. There is also a café.

4. Feinkost Käfer
🗺 H4 📍 Prinzregentenstraße 73
Catering king Gerd Käfer's Bogenhausen delicatessen is the place where celebrities come to do their food shopping.

5. Doppler Shop
🗺 G5 📍 Metzstraße 15 (entrance on Sedanstraße)
This is the place for quirky and unique homeware, from stationery through to tableware and cushions.

6. Kokolores
🗺 G5 📍 Wörthstraße 8
This is a shop filled with interesting finds, from colourful postcards and stationery through to unique gifts, including tin toys and robots.

7. The Lovely Concept
🗺 G5 📍 Steinstraße 27
A modern store selling quirky clothing and accessories plus a variety of interior decor items.

8. Mohrmann Basics
🗺 Q4 📍 Innere Wiener Straße 50
Striking fashion that's anything but ordinary – this small shop attracts customers to Haidhausen from miles around. Mohrmann stocks a wide range of different labels.

9. Buch & Töne
🗺 G6 📍 Weißenburger Str. 14
A charming bookshop stocking a mix of new and second-hand books, along with with audiobooks and a selection of CDs.

10. Markt am Wiener Platz
🗺 Q4
The permanent market stalls at Wiener Platz are open on weekdays and sell exquisite foodstuffs, from Alpine cheeses to Greek olives. It's a lovely place to stop for a coffee too.

Cafés and Pubs

1. True & 12
G5 **Rosenheimer Straße 14** **Winter**

Sample 12 different flavours of ice cream at this small parlour. It uses high-quality ingredients; the hazelnuts are imported from Piedmont, and the milk is sourced from a farm just outside of Munich.

2. Negroni
G5 **Sedanstraße 9** **Sun**

Great cocktails are the order of the day at this American-style bar. The unpretentious menu features Italian-inspired cuisine.

3. Barroom
G5 **Milchstraße 17** **Sun & Mon**

The smallest cocktail bar in Munich, this venue specializes in rum-based concoctions. Expect it to be busy.

4. Café la Maison
G6 **Weißenburger Straße 6**

Laidback, French café with a large cobbled terrace. Its delicacies include tasty vegan pastries and cakes.

5. Café im Hinterhof
G5 **Sedanstraße 29**

This Art Nouveau-style café serves a generous breakfast. There's a quiet terrace in the inner courtyard.

6. Fortuna Cafebar
G5 **Sedanstraße 18**

This small neighbourhood café with an Italian feel has tables both inside and out. It's an excellent place to come for Sunday brunch, and the hot chocolate is to die for.

7. Café Hüller
F6 **Eduard-Schmid-Straße 8**

This neighbourhood café is located in a pretty spot near the Isar river.

8. POLKA Bar
G6 **Pariser Straße 38** **Sun & Mon**

Set in a basement vault, this bar is the perfect place to unwind and listen to music over a drink.

9. Johanniscafé
G5 **Johannisplatz 15**

This café is in a time-warped world of its own, with an old-fashioned interior that include a retro jukebox.

10. Lollo Rosso
G5 **Milchstraße 1** **Sun–Tue**

The so-called Bar(varian) Grill serves up a combination of Mediterranean and Bavarian favourites, from steaks to snacks, and a long list of drinks.

Entrance to the Café Hüller

Places to Eat

Two diners enjoying a meal at the Chez Fritz

to enjoy pizza and pasta. Outdoor seating is available if the weather is good.

1. Chopan am Gasteig
G5 Rosenheimer Straße 8
chopan-am-gasteig.de · €€
Munich has one of the largest Afghan communities in Europe, and this stylish restaurant is a good option to try traditional Afghan cuisine.

2. Nana
Q5 Metzstraße 15
nana-muenchen.de · €
Bringing a touch of Tel Aviv to Munich, Nana serves great mezzes.

3. Le Faubourg
G5 Kirchenstraße 5 Sun & Mon le-faubourg.de · €€
Le Faubourg offers a bistro atmosphere complete with bijou tables and specials presented on a chalkboard, plus an excellent wine selection. A limited number of outdoor tables are available.

4. Rue des Halles
G5 Steinstraße 18 Mon & Tue rue-des-halles.de · €€€
The oldest French restaurant in Munich offers classic cooking at its finest.

5. Il Cigno
H5 Wörthstraße 39
(089) 448 5589 Sun · €
Italian food is incredibly popular in Munich and Il Cigno is a great place

6. Vinaiolo
G5 Steinstraße 42
Sun vinaiolo.de · €€€
A Haidhausen favourite, this restaurant has a shop-like dining space and Mediterranean dishes on the menu.

7. Chez Fritz
G5 Preysingstraße 20
Sun & Mon chezfritz.de · €€
This brasserie offers an upscale French menu with a retro atmosphere. Tables available on Preysingplatz.

8. Bernard et Bernard
G5 Innere Wienerstraße 32
Sun creperie-bernard.de · €
What this crêperie lacks in size, it more than makes up for in quality, serving tasty crêpes, galettes and Breton-inspired dishes.

9. Zum Kloster
G5 Preysingstraße 77
zumkloster-muenchen.de · €
This rustic restaurant is the place to go for organic home cooking. Outdoor seating is available beneath cherry trees on a quiet street.

10. PreysingGarten
G5 Preysingstraße 69
preysinggarten.com · €
Breakfast (until 3pm), lunch and dinner are served Italian style at this wood-panelled venue. It also has an attractive garden and play area.

SOUTH WEST

The area to the west and south of the Old Town is diverse and surprisingly green. Ludwigsvorstadt is the site of the huge Hauptbahnhof (Munich's main railway station) and Theresienwiese, the venue for the annual Oktoberfest. To the south of Sendlinger Tor and the Gärtnerplatz quarter, Isarvorstadt is home to a large number of independent shops and lively cafés, while the nearby Isar riverbanks offer great riverside walks with a picturesque backdrop. While the southwestern corner of this part of Munich is home to the sprawling Westpark, the Westend area, west of Theresienwiese, is a multi-cultural quarter that is undergoing rapid change. This densely built district is also home to attractions such as Munich's oldest brewery (Augustiner), the former chief customs office and several beautiful green public spaces, including the statue-filled Bavariapark.

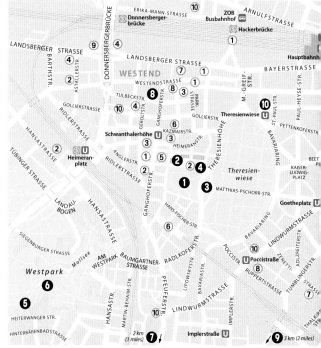

For places to stay in this area, see p148

Relaxing by the trees in the lush Bavariapark

1 Bavariapark
D5

The park directly behind the Bavaria statue dates back to Ludwig I, who commissioned the creation of the "Theresienhain" (as it was then known) at the start of the 19th century. In 1872, the park was opened to the public and it later became an exhibition space when the Alte Messe events venue was established. Today, locals enjoy the park as somewhere to go jogging or to simply relax. It is home to a number of old stone sculptures as well as the Wirtshaus am Bavariapark *(p123)*.

2 Altes Messegelände and Verkehrszentrum
D5 Am Bavariapark 5

The former site of the Alte Messe (Old Fair) underwent massive development when the trade fair moved to its current location in Riem. Contemporary residences were built, including the tower of the Steidle-Haus, and the exhibition halls were converted for cultural use. The Verkehrszentrum (a branch of the Deutsches Museum; *p34*), which chronicles the history of transport, is housed here in three Art Nouveau halls. Its permanent exhibition divides its collection of vehicles into three themes: urban transport, travel and technology.

3 Bavaria Statue and Theresienwiese
D5 Theresienhöhe 16
Apr–mid-Oct: 9am–6pm daily (Ohtoberfest: to 8pm)

Standing 18.5 m (61 ft) tall, the bronze statue of Bavaria towers over her surroundings and has an observation platform inside her head. Leo von Klenze's Ruhmeshalle (Hall of Fame), with busts honouring famous Bavarians, stands behind the colossal figure. Bavaria overlooks Theresienwiese, home of many events – most notably the Oktoberfest *(p42)*. A festival was held here on 12 October 1810 to celebrate the wedding of crown prince Ludwig and Therese von Sachsen-Hildburghausen. In honour of the bride, the festival ground was named Theresienwiese.

Iconic statue of Bavaria

Alter Botanischer Garten
ELISENSTR.
MAYERSTR. KARLS-PLATZ
arlsplatz
HRSTR.
SONNENSTRASSE
BAUMSTR.
Sendlinger Tor
IRMSTRASSE
THALKIRCHNER STRASSE
BLUMENSTR.
FRAUNHOFERSTR.
CORNELIUS-STR.
GÄRTNER-PLATZ STR.
PESTALOZZISTRASSE
KLENZESTR.
ICKSTATT-STR.
HOLZSTR.
AM GLOCKENBACH
ISARVORSTADT
Fraunhofer-straße
NERSTR.
WITTELSBACHERSTR.
BALDE-PLATZ
Wittelsbacher-brücke
EDUARD-SCHMID-STR.
SCHYREN-PLATZ
ASAMSTR.
ENTENBACHSTR.
Isar
ROECKL-PLATZ

0 metres 500
0 yards 500

Stunning Thai pavilion at the Westpark

4 Alte Kongresshalle
D5 · **Theresienhöhe 15**
Built in 1952–3 in retro-futuristic style, the Old Congress Hall is one of a number of buildings that survived from the former exhibition grounds. Equipped with state-of-the-art technology, it often hosts cultural and social events. The hall's former teahouse is home to the Kongress Bar, while the Wirtshaus am Bavariapark *(p123)* can be found at the south end of the site.

5 Sardenhaus
C6 · **Heiterwanger Str. 46**
Built in the style of a traditional Sardinian stone house, the tranquil Sardenhaus was created for the 1983 International Garden Expo. A welcome oasis, its roof is covered with wildflowers, and many visit this spot to escape the hustle and bustle of the city and enjoy nature. It often hosts regularly changing exhibitions run by local artists. There's also a popular playground nearby.

6 Westpark
B6
A smaller, Westend version of the Englischer Garten, the Westpark was created for the fourth International Horticultural Exposition in 1983. Among its attractions are landscaped gardens, barbecue and picnic facilities, two large lakes, and two beer gardens. The Asian section with its Japanese garden and Thai *sala* (pavilion) is especially beautiful.

7 DAV Kletter- und Boulderzentrum
D7 · **Thalkirchner Straße 207** · **7am–11pm Mon–Fri, 8am–11pm Sat & Sun** · **kbthalkirchen.de**
One of the biggest climbing spots in Munich, this centre opened a state-of-the-art bouldering area in 2024. There's an outdoor children's play area as well as several indoor climbing walls for kids. It has an on-site café, which serves excellent pizza and coffee.

8 Westend
C5–D5
The Westend area, which is officially known as Schwanthalerhöhe after sculptor Ludwig von Schwanthaler, developed with the start of industrialization. Schwanthaler designed the Bavaria statue, a masterpiece cast by Ferdinand von Miller from 1840 to 1850. This section of the city was long considered a "Glasscherbenviertel" (broken glass, or pub district) with a multicultural vibe, but is now a real mix of old and new. The relocation of the trade fair gave rise to the construction

of new residential areas, although the neighbourhood still retains some original buildings. Traditional pubs and shops sit beside chic cafés and stylish boutiques. This area around the Hauptbahnhof is particularly lively due to its flourishing immigrant communities, who have opened up a variety of shops and cafés here.

9 Flaucher
E7

This is Munich's best beach by the Isar. Every summer, sun worshippers flock to the gravel banks along the southern Isar, and many stop in at the pretty beer garden of the same name.

10 Paulskirche
E5 **St-Pauls-Platz 11**

The view over the Wiesn (annual site of the Oktoberfest) from the 97-m (318-ft) high tower of this Neo-Gothic church is simply glorious, once you've climbed the 252 steps. St Paul's was the scene of tragic events in 1960, when a US military aircraft hit the tower and crashed down on a tram, shortly after take-off from Munich-Riem airport.

Neo-Gothic façade of the Paulskirche

A DAY IN WESTEND

Morning

Begin at the **Bavaria** statue (p117). Climb up and enjoy the view across Theresienwiese. Behind the Ruhmeshalle is the **Bavariapark** (p117). Walk to its northern end to visit the **Verkehrszentrum** (p117), a branch of the Deutsches Museum. Cross Heimeranstraße and follow the tree-lined passage to Kazmairstraße (check out the sgraffito at No 21). A few houses further down on the left, you'll find **SchokoAlm** (Kazmairstraße 33), which serves delicious coffee, cocoa, chocolates, gingerbread and cake. Next, stroll through the Westend quarter from **Gollierplatz** (p120) to **Georg-Freundorfer-Platz** (p120). For lunch, try **Marais** (p121) or **La Kaz** (p123).

Afternoon

Head back through Bavariapark, and across the Quartiersplatz Theresienhöhe (over the S-Bahn) to reach the **Westpark**. Stroll westwards until you come to the "**Die Arche**" installation by Steffen Schuster, with a whole host of colourful animals. Making your way past the turtles in the **Mollsee**, past the **Audi Dome** and over the bridge (Mittlerer Ring), you will soon reach the western section of the park, which is home to a Thai sala, Chinese and Japanese garden, rose garden and a lake with a stage for open-air performances. If you're ready for a beer and a snack, call in at the **Wirtshaus am Rosengarten** restaurant (Westendstraße 305).

The Best of the Rest

1. Hackerbrücke
📍 K3
One of the few wrought-iron arch bridges in Germany, the Hackerbrücke crosses the tracks in front of the Hauptbahnhof (train station; also the site of the central bus terminal).

2. ADAC Zentrale
📍 C5 🏠 Hansastraße 19
This showstopper Westend building (93 m/305 ft tall) features over 1,000 windows that shimmer in 22 colours. It is home to ADAC, the German motoring organization.

3. Georg-Freundorfer-Platz
📍 D5
This square with a football pitch, summer curling and a climbing garden is a popular hangout for families.

4. Central Tower
📍 D4 🏠 Landsberger Straße 110
This distinctive, 23-storey building is one of Munich's few skyscrapers.

5. Endlose Treppe
📍 D5 🏠 Ganghoferstraße 29
Olafur Eliasson's *Endlose Treppe* (Endless Staircase) is located in the courtyard of the KPMG offices.

6. Quartiersplatz Theresienhöhe
📍 D6
This pretty concrete ceiling above the railway tracks was designed in 2010 as a landscape sculpture, complete with hills, dunes and a play area ideal for older kids.

7. Augustiner-Bräu
📍 D4 🏠 Landsberger Straße 35
Munich's oldest brand of beer is brewed in the brickwork Augustiner brewery, which also has its own beer hall called the Augustiner Bräustuben (*p123*).

8. Alter Südfriedhof
📍 E6
Many prominent figures are buried at the city's oldest central cemetery. Today, local residents like to take a stroll under its ancient trees.

9. Hauptzollamt
📍 C4 🏠 Landsberger Straße 124
The main customs office, with its Jugendstil elements and glass dome, dates back to 1912.

10. Gollierplatz
📍 D5
This beautiful, tree-lined square at the heart of Westend features a number of Jugendstil houses and the Neo-Romanesque St Rupert's church.

Eliasson's *Endlose Treppe* in the KPMG office

Cafés and Pubs

Outdoor tables at the French-inspired Marais

1. Cafe Simurg
📍 D5 🏠 Sandtnerstraße 5
This former grocery shop is now a café that still retains some of its old charm. Good cakes, as well as breakfast and salads.

2. Café Westend
📍 D5 🏠 Ganghoferstraße 50
This combined café, bar and restaurant serves a great-value business lunch. It also has pool tables and bowling alleys in the basement.

3. Marais
📍 D5 🏠 Parhstraße 2
A former shop with a nostalgic interior, including wooden chests and toy prams. Guests can drink coffee in the window display.

4. Café am Beethovenplatz
📍 E5 🏠 Goethestraße 51
This traditional café, in a listed Belle Époque house belonging to the Hotel Mariandl *(p148)*, offers a real taste of Viennese coffee-house culture. There is live classical or jazz music every day and a small garden to enjoy in summer.

5. Café Lozzi
📍 E5 🏠 Pestalozzistraße 8
A charming café close to the Sendlinger Tor, Café Lozzi features vintage decor

and plenty of vegan options. It draws a young crowd and has a great outdoor seating area.

6. München 72
📍 E5 🏠 Holzstraße 16 🔒 Mon
Named in memory of the attack at the 1972 Olympics, this café bar is brimming with 1970s' furnishings – including a bicycle hanging behind the bar. München 72 draws in a varied crowd in the evening. The long-running German TV crime show *Tatort* is screened here on Sundays.

7. Tagträumer
📍 E6 🏠 Dreimühlenstraße 17
🔒 Sun & Mon
This coffee shop in the Schlachthof Quarter is steeped in history – it was previously a police station and a butcher's shop, to name just two of its former incarnations – and is an atmospheric place for breakfast.

8. Substanz
📍 E6 🏠 Ruppertstraße 28
This long-established pub, bar and live club hosts famous bands and newcomers alike, not to mention monthly poetry slams. It's very popular, so arrive early to get a seat.

9. Ferdings
📍 F5 🏠 Klenzestraße 43
🔒 Sun & Mon
Don't be put off by the bathrobes in the cloakroom – they are provided to keep smokers warm outside. This industrial bar serves regional tapas and a great selection of drinks.

10. bean batter
📍 D5 🏠 Schwanthalerstraße 123
Serving speciality coffee, sweet treats and great comfort food, this laidback café is popular with coffee lovers. The stars of the show are definitely the freshly baked Belgian waffles.

Shops

**Colourful trinkets on offer
at Roly Poly**

1. Parke6
📍 D5 📍 Schwanthalerstraße 156

A stylish concept store selling vintage fashion and accessories.

2. WARE FREUDE
📍 C5 📍 Westendstraße 142

Perfect for souvenir shopping, this place sells T-shirts, postcards and decorative items. The brand is synonymous with regional design and ecological production.

3. SchokoAlm
📍 D5 📍 Kazmairstraße 33

When it comes to chocolate, this chocolatier offers everything you could dream of and more, including tempting truffles, sweets and pastries, and gorgeous cakes. It also has its own café with limited outdoor seating.

4. Kunst und Keramik Muck
📍 D5 📍 Bergmannstraße 29

Set off Gollierplatz, this studio features handmade ceramic pieces by artist Lisa Muck. Pottery courses are also available for those keen to learn.

5. Roly Poly
📍 F5 📍 Fraunhoferstraße 9

This designer fabric shop sells organic materials and accessories for both adults and kids. It also offers sewing courses. If you're interested in needlecraft, then Roly Poly is definitely worth a visit.

6. Götterspeise
📍 F6 📍 Jahnstraße 30

The best hang-out for chocolate fans, this shop offers a whole host of tasty treats, vegan and lactose-free goodies, and gifts. The café serves cakes, pastries and coffee.

7. Antonetty
📍 F6 📍 Klenzestraße 56

Bags, clothes and a variety of other items made of leather are to be found in this shop. The little leather animals make good gifts.

8. Rocket
📍 F5 📍 Reichenbachstraße 41

This shop stocks the latest streetwear, shoes, accessories, bags and jewellery for adults and children.

9. Wohnpalette
📍 F5 📍 Reichenbachstraße 28

Visit Wohnpalette if you're shopping for picture frames, metal signs, decorative lighting or candlesticks.

10. ReSales
📍 D6 📍 Lindwurmstraße 82

Located to the south of the Theresienwiese, this shop sells good-quality vintage and second-hand clothing.

**Lovely window display
at Götterspeise**

Industrial chic decor at La Kaz

Places to Eat

1. Augustiner Bräustuben
📍 D4 🏠 Landsberger Straße 19
🌐 braeustuben.de · €
A traditional Bavarian tavern at the heart of the Augustiner brewery.

2. Wirtshaus am Bavariapark
📍 D5 🏠 Theresienhöhe 15
🌐 wirtshaus-am-bavariapark.com · €
A great pub with a beer garden at the edge of Bavariapark.

3. Junge Römer
📍 E5 🏠 Pestalozzistraße 23
🚫 Mon 🌐 jungeroemer-muenchen.de · €
An Italian restaurant with a large selection of pasta and *pinsa* (a type of pizza with less salt).

4. Wirtshaus Eder
📍 C5 🏠 Gollierstraße 83
🌐 ederwirt.de · €
Enjoy craft beers on tap at this Bavarian pub. Try the spinach dumplings.

5. Paulaner Bräuhaus
📍 E6 🏠 Kapuzinerplatz 5
🌐 paulaner-brauhaus.de · €
This traditional brewery tavern has a bar, lounge areas and a beer garden.

6. La Kaz
📍 D5 🏠 Ligsalzstraße 38 🚫 L, Mon–Fri 🌐 lakaz.jimdo.com · €
Customers at this popular, independently owned pub perch

on colourful stools at wooden tables to enjoy well-chilled wines and excellent food.

7. Wirtshaus im Schlachthof
📍 E6 🏠 Zenettistraße 9 🚫 L & Tue
🌐 im-schlachthof.de · €
This tavern with a beer garden and stage hosts a range of events.

8. Zur Schwalbe
📍 D5 🏠 Schwanthalerstraße 149
🌐 zurschwalbe.com · €€
Try dishes from the Alps here, such as pretzel salad or mountain cheese dumplings.

9. La Vecchia Masseria
📍 L4 🏠 Mathildenstraße 3
🌐 lavecchiamasseria.de · €
Arguably the best Italian restaurant in town, La Veccia serves traditional dishes in a warm and welcoming atmosphere.

10. Stemmerhof
📍 D6 🏠 Plinganserstraße 6
🚫 Sun 🌐 stemmerhof.de · €€
This urban yet rural place in a former farmyard serves European favourites.

NORTH WEST

West of Maxvorstadt, Munich's northwest includes the districts of Neuhausen and Nymphenburg. The vast Hirschgarten – the world's largest beer garden and a must visit whether you love beer or not – is located in the far west of this part of the city and is populated with wild deer. The Olympiapark, home to the 1972 Olympic Games, and its varied attractions are located to the north, neighbouring one of Munich's largest companies, BMW, whose museum and BMW Welt attractions lie close to the car-maker's state-of-the-art plant.

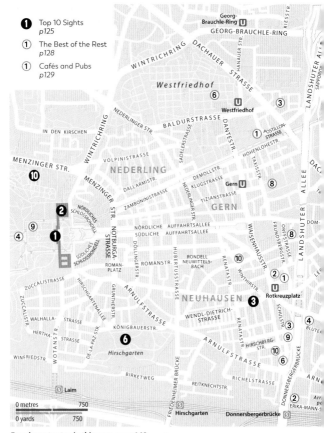

1 Top 10 Sights
p125

1 The Best of the Rest
p128

1 Cafés and Pubs
p129

For places to stay in this area, see p149

Striking façade of the Schloss Nymphenburg

1 Schloss Nymphenburg

Originally built as the 17th-century summer palace of Elector Ferdinand and Adelaide of Savoy, but much expanded since, Schloss Nymphenburg *(p38)* is one of the best places to escape the bustle of the city centre. Once you've toured the palace's many rooms, spend some time in the magnificent landscaped gardens, which are dotted with pavilions. Nymphenburg is famous for its porcelain, and a factory shop is located just outside the Schloss entrance. There are also a couple of museums in the palace wings that are worth a visit. There's also a café-restaurant *(p128)* where you can refuel.

2 Museum Mensch und Natur

📍 B2 🏛 Schloss Nymphenburg
🕐 9am–5pm Tue–Fri, 10am–6pm Sat & Sun 🖥 mmn-muenchen.snsb.de 🌐

Located in a separate wing of the Schloss Nymphenburg, this museum guides you on a journey through biological, earth and life sciences, as you discover the history of Earth and life as we know it through dioramas, natural objects and interactive exhibits. One of the real stars of the exhibition is Bruno, the bear who wandered over the Alps into Bavaria from Italy in 2006 and was ultimately shot, despite protests.

3 Neuhausen

📍 C3

Rotkreuzplatz is the centre of Munich's second-largest urban district, with myriad bars and restaurants lining the streets surrounding the square. The many old buildings make it a popular residential area, and the quality of life here is excellent thanks to the multitude of green spaces such as the Botanischer Garten, Schlosspark Nymphenburg and the Hirschgarten.

**Vintage Isetta car,
BMW Museum**

4 BMW Museum

📍 E1 📌 Am Olympiapark 2
🕐 10am–6pm Tue–Sun 🌐 bmw-welt.com 🔗

At the foot of the four-cylinder BMW Headquarters lies the bowl-shaped BMW Museum. This flat-roofed building is home to a permanent exhibition featuring over 120 cars, motorbikes and engines spanning over a century of BMW history, while the "bowl" hosts changing exhibits.

5 BMW Welt

📍 E1 📌 Am Olympiapark 1
🕐 7:30am–midnight daily (from 9am Sun); exhibitions: 9am–6pm daily 🌐 bmw-welt.com

This prestigious BMW building has been a prominent feature at the Olympiapark since 2007. As the car manufacturer's distribution and experience centre, it has become one of the most popular attractions in Munich. Its distinctive double-cone design houses several exhibitions, as well as hosting political, art and cultural events. In addition to its many shops, you can find several restaurants here, including the Michelin-starred EssZimmer (*(089) 3 5899 1814*) – home of top chef Bobby Bräuer.

6 Hirschgarten

📍 B3–4 📌 Hirschgarten 1
🕐 10am–midnight daily (beer garden: from 11:30am) 🌐 hirschgarten.de

To the south of Schloss Nymphenburg, this beer garden is home to its own fallow deer enclosure, a nod to the park's former function as a hunting ground (from 1780) for the Elector Carl Theodor. A new hunting lodge was built in 1791 and became a popular destination for locals – particularly when it was licensed to sell beer. This was the first step in the venue becoming the tavern it is today, although it's probably best known for its huge beer garden (Bavaria's largest) where customers enjoy Augustiner beer in the shade of the chestnut trees. The 40-ha (99-acre) park is a much-loved site for sport and relaxation, including playgrounds, hills for tobogganing, and barbecue pits.

7 Circus Krone

📍 D4 📌 Zirkus-Krone-Straße 1–6
🌐 circus-krone.com

While the circus tours in the summer, the Circus Krone Building hosts concerts and other events. Circus season

Ultra-modern structure of the BMW Welt

Stars in the Ring performing at Circus Krone

traditionally begins on Christmas Day and offers three different shows until the end of February.

8 Sea Life

🔲 E1 📍 Willi-Daume-Platz 1 🕐 10am–7pm daily 🌐 visitsealife.com ↗

This aquarium can be found at the Olympiapark and is a popular destination for visitors of all ages. One of the highlights is the shark tunnel.

9 Olympiapark

Created in north Schwabing for the 1972 Summer Olympics, this site (*p40*) is the top sport and recreational ground in Munich.

10 Botanischer Garten

🔲 A2 📍 Menzinger Straße 65 🕐 Hours vary, chech website 🌐 botmuc.de ↗

Around 19,500 plant species from across the globe are cultivated outdoors and in greenhouses in these botanical gardens, which were laid out at the start of the 20th century. Highlights here include the Alpinum and its alpine flora, the Arboretum with rare trees from around the world, June's spectacular rhododendron display, the fern glen and an insect pavilion full of butterflies. The impressive greenhouses shelter tropical plants, cacti and fruit trees, unusual orchids and giant water lilies.

A DAY IN THE NORTH WEST

Morning

Start the day at **Schloss Nymphenburg** (*p38*). Depending on the weather, you can enjoy a stroll through the Schlosspark or marvel at the palace interior. For a coffee break, head into the **Schlosscafé im Palmenhaus** (*p128*). Note that Nymphenburg is home to interesting museums, such as the **Museum Mensch und Natur** (*p125*). Once you're done here, wander down Auffahrtsallee towards Nymphenburger Straße and stop for lunch at the **Volkart** (*p129*) tapas bar on Volkartstraße.

Afternoon

From Nymphenburger Straße, it isn't far to **Rotkreuzplatz**. From here, take tram 12 (towards Scheidplatz) as far as Infanteriestraße and head down Ackermannstraße. You'll reach the **Olympiapark** where you can admire at the architecture of the Olympic buildings. Take in the view from the **Olympiaturm** tower – on a clear day you'll be able to see distant mountains. Once you've made your way back down, there's plenty more exciting architecture to enjoy, with **BMW Welt** waiting for you on the other side of the street. There's even the opportunity to make a quick detour to the **BMW Museum**, if you're interested. After a busy day's sightseeing, you can round things off at the exquisite EssZimmer restaurant at BMW Welt.

The Best of the Rest

1. Dantebad
C2 ☐ Postillonstraße 17 ☐ Hours vary, check website ☐ swm.de
This open-air facility has more pools than any other swimming site in Munich. It also has heated outdoor pools.

2. Freiheiz
D4 ☐ Rainer-Werner-Fassbinder-Platz 1
The renovated hall of this former thermal power station is a popular venue for concerts and events.

3. Borstei
D1 ☐ Dachauer Straße 140
Built in 1924–9 as an alternative to house sharing, this residential area has court-yards, gardens, fountains and a museum.

4. Nymphenburger Kanal
A3
Commissioned by Max Emanuel in 1701, the Nympenburger canal is a popular spot for curling when it freezes over in winter.

5. Utopia
E3 ☐ Heßstraße 132
These Neo-Romanesque former stables are now used to host events

Colourful buildings, Borstei housing complex

Bustling beer garden at Augustiner-Keller

including theatre performances, concerts and the Opernfestspiele.

6. Westfriedhof
C1 ☐ Baldurstraße 28
A quiet cemetery where the likes of art collector Franz von Lenbach (p95) and artist Peter Halm are buried.

7. Augustiner-Keller
D4 ☐ Arnulfstraße 52
This historic restaurant has a beer garden filled with old chestnut trees. Augustiner Edelstoff is served on tap.

8. Taxisgarten
C2 ☐ Taxisstraße 12
Established in 1924, this relaxed beer garden hosts brass band per-formances at weekends.

9. Schlosscafé im Palmenhaus
A3 ☐ Schloss Nymphenburg, entrance 43 ☐ 11am–6pm daily ☐ palmenhaus.de
A former greenhouse, this building is now a bright and airy café-restaurant with tables in the garden.

10. Herz-Jesu-Kirche
C3 ☐ Lachnerstraße 8
Built in the late 1990s, this church resembles a semi-transparent cube with a blue front. The interior features a free-standing wooden cube with slats that create different light effects.

Cafés and Pubs

1. The Victorian House
📍 C3 🏠 Ysenburgstraße 13 🕐 Sun eve, Mon & Tue 🌐 victorianhouse.de

A British venue offering a fusion of new and traditional English cuisine from breakfast to dinner. Take a seat on the terrace and enjoy the afternoon tea.

2. Volkart
📍 C3 🏠 Volkartstraße 15 🕐 L, Mon & Sun 🌐 volk-art.com

Tapas and Mexican cuisine are what it's all about here, including a wide variety of vegetarian options. Outdoor tables are available.

3. Kitchen2Soul
📍 C3 🏠 Schlörstraße 1 🕐 Sun–Wed 🌐 kitchen2soul.com

This cute café also operates as an independent bookstore. Breakfast here is a highlight, with muesli, avocado toast and fresh pastries on offer. Kitchen2Soul also hosts seminars, creative workshops and training courses.

4. Café Neuhausen
📍 D3 🏠 Blutenburgstraße 106 🌐 dasneuhausen.de

This café, with a stuccoed ceiling and a covered garden, serves breakfast, lunch and dinner (plus Sunday brunch). The menu comprises Italian, Austrian and Bavarian dishes.

5. Café Kosmos
📍 L2 🏠 Dachauer Straße 7 🕐 Sat & Sun L 🌐 cafe-kosmos.de

Situated by the Hauptbahnhof, this bar with a retro charm has a spiral staircase. It is normally very busy, so be prepared to wait.

6. Piacere Nuovo
📍 C4 🏠 Donnersbergerstraße 54 🕐 Sat & Sun 🌐 piacere-nuovo.com

With delicious homemade Italian specialities and wonderfully friendly service, Piacere Nuovo is a fabulous place for both lunch and dinner.

7. Butter
📍 D3 🏠 Blutenburgstraße 90 🕐 Sat & Sun

A great little bistro serving breakfast, pastries and flavoursome mains.

8. Café Ruffini
📍 D3 🏠 Orffstraße 22–4 🕐 Mon 🌐 ruffini.de

The city's first eco café, this venue offers organic treats, including breakfasts and baked goods from its own bakery. Sit on the rooftop terrace, where readings are occasionally held.

9. MARITA
📍 C3 🏠 Schulstraße 34 🕐 Sun & Mon 🌐 marita-cafe.de

A pretty little café with outdoor seating, MARITA offers a long, varied breakfast and lunch menu and locally baked cakes.

10. Sappralott
📍 C3 🏠 Donnersbergerstraße 37 🌐 sappralott.de

An Augustinian guesthouse with dark wood panelling, Sappralott serves Bavarian and international cuisine. Happy hour is from 11pm.

Patrons enjoying a meal, The Victorian House

BEYOND MUNICH

Munich is the ideal starting point for excursions to the Bavarian Alps. With excellent slopes and the many ski lifts and shelters, the Alps offer ideal conditions for skiers, while the many lakes, such as those in Upper Bavaria – Ammersee and Starnberger See – draw watersports enthusiasts and ice-skaters, while the mountains are filled with hikers during the summer. It's worth noting that the Alps aren't just for hikers and sports enthusiasts; you can reach Germany's highest peak – Zugspitze – in a day, via the mountain railway and cable car. Also within easy reach are a number of ancient monasteries and world-famous churches, including the Wieskirche, a UNESCO World Heritage Site. A visit to at least one of Ludwig's palaces, preferably Neuschwanstein, is essential. Lower Bavaria, bordering Austria and the Czech Republic in the east, is a peaceful oasis with charmingly preserved towns, including Lanshut and Passau.

For places to stay in this area, see p149

Admiring the Zugspitze from the observation platform

1 Zugspitze

One of the best ways to enjoy the Zugspitze is to take a round trip on the mountain train and cable car. In Garmisch, the journey begins with the funicular, which takes you to the Schneeferner glacier on the Zugspitzplatt. Here, you switch to a cable car, which ascends to the summit. The observation platform offers a spectacular vista, and on a clear day you can see all the way to the Dolomites. Take the cable car on your way back down to the valley, and you'll be treated to wonderful views of Eibsee, Garmisch-Partenkirchen and Werdenfelser Land.

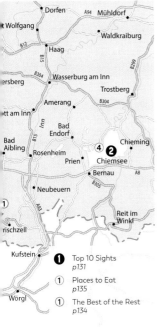

2 Chiemsee, Herrenchiemsee and Fraueninsel

Popularly thought of as the "Bavarian Sea", Chiemsee is Bavaria's largest lake, with an area of 80 sq km (31 sq miles). It is home to four islands, the largest of which are Herreninsel and Fraueninsel – the latter has an 8th-century monastery. It is at Herrenchiemsee that you will find the Altes Schloss, an Augustinian monastery, and the Neues Schloss (Schloss Herrenchiemsee), which is said to be Ludwig II's Bavarian equivalent of Versailles. Despite construction beginning in 1878, the Neues Schloss was never completed. Its extravagant staircase and large mirror gallery are particularly impressive. The south wing is home to the King Ludwig II Museum (open daily, see herrenchiemsee.de for details).

3 Schloss Linderhof

◻ Linderhof 12, Ettal ◻ Apr–mid-Oct: 9am–6pm daily; mid-Oct–Mar: 10am–4:30pm daily ⬤ schlosslinderhof.de ◻

Of all Ludwig II's fairytale residences, Schloss Linderhof best shows his great fondness for France and his regard for the Bourbons and Louis XIV. The palace was originally a hunting lodge belonging to Maximilian II. Ludwig II had it torn down and rebuilt in the park, making it the only palace that was actually completed during his lifetime. The Schlosspark comprises a French garden complete with parterres and terraces, surrounded by a country park. It is home to attractions such as the Marokkanische Haus, Maurische Kiosk, and the famous Venus Grotto, where the king liked to be rowed around in a golden boat.

Golden fountain at the Schloss Linderhof

4 Wieskirche

◻ Wies 14, Steingaden ◻ 8am–8pm daily (winter: to 5pm) ⬤ wieskirche.de

Known simply as the Wieskirche, the mid-18th-century Pilgrim Church of the Scourged Saviour is renowned as a prime example of German Rococo. It represents the work of Dominikus Zimmermann at his peak. UNESCO listed the church as a World Heritage Site in 1983.

5 Kloster Andechs

⬤ andechs.de

This "holy mountain" stands almost 200 m (656 ft) tall on the east bank of the Ammersee. Founded in 1455 as a Dominican monastery with a Rococo church, it is one of the most significant pilgrimage sites in Bavaria. Its tavern and beer garden attract crowds wanting to try the famous monastery beer, Andechser.

6 Starnberger See

Of all the lakes in this area, it was Starnberger See (21 km/13 miles long, 5 km/3 miles wide and up to 127 m/417 ft deep) that became the most popular with the local poplation. Just like Ammersee, Tegernsee and Königssee, this lake is also home to tour boats from the "Weißblaue Flotte" fleet. Featuring a beautiful rose garden, the Roseninsel is the only island in the middle of

Splendid Rococo interior of the Wieskirche

the lake and can be easily reached with smaller boats. The lake itself is surrounded by a number of palaces: "Sisi-Schloss" Possenhofen, Tutzing, Ammerland, and Berg, which was the summer house of the Wittelsbachs. It was near Berg that Ludwig II died under mysterious circumstances just a few metres from the shore, and a memorial cross marks the tragic spot in the lake. The Expressionist collection at the Buchheim Museum (the Museum der Phantasie), north of Bernried, is well worth a visit.

7 Garmisch-Partenkirchen

Located at the base of the Wetterstein massif and the Zugspitze, the capital of Werdenfelser Land is one of the most popular winter sports resorts in the country, with a convenient motorway link to Munich. In fact, the Winter Olympics were held here in 1936, as were the FIS Alpine World Ski Championships in 1978, 2011 and 2024. The buzzing spa town also draws a large number of visitors during the summer months, as its prime location makes it an ideal base for mountain hiking and excursions into the wider region. The town is light on sights, but the main draw here is without doubt the train and cable car ride up the Zugspitze. A road south of Partenkirchen leads to the scenic Partnach river gorge (Partnachklamm). Further along, an uphill walk of several hours leads to Ludwig II's hunting lodge in Schachen.

8 Neuschwanstein

Ludwig II's fairytale castle (p44) is one of the most popular in Europe and well worth a visit.

9 Ammersee

The third-largest lake in Bavaria, Ammersee occupies a glacial basin dating from the Ice Age. On a clear day, the view of the Alps is breathtaking. A variety of activities are available around the banks of the lake, including sailing, rowing, surfing, diving, cycling and walking.

10 Tegernsee and Schliersee

Framed by wooded mountains, Tegernsee is one of the largest mountain lakes in Upper Bavaria, with an area of 9 sq km (3.5 sq miles). Its beautiful setting and proximity to Munich have made it a perennially popular holiday destination.

Strolling along the picturesque Tegernsee

The Best of the Rest

**Inner courtyard at
Kloster Benediktbeuern**

1. Wendelstein
This 1838-m (6030-ft) mountain peak can be reached via the 1912 rack railway, by cable car or on foot.

2. Spitzingsee
This romantic lake is in the Spitzingsee–Tegernsee ski resort.

3. Münter-Haus, Murnau
⬜ Kottmüllerallee 6, Murnau
🕐 2–5pm Tue–Sun ⬜
The Münter-Haus was the summer house of Gabriele Münter and Wassily Kandinsky, and a meeting point for the "Blue Rider" artists.

4. Kloster Benediktbeuern
⬜ Don-Bosco-Straße 1, Benediktbeuern ⬜
Benediktbeuern Abbey is one of the oldest monasteries in Germany, dating from 739 CE. The library in the present Baroque complex was once home to the 13th-century *Carmina Burana* manuscript. Tours take place on Thursday, Saturday and Sunday.

5. Kloster Ettal
⬜ Kaiser-Ludwig-Platz 1, Ettal
Now a boarding school, this abbey is famous for its herbal liqueur (which can still be bought here).

6. Dachau
⬜ Alte Römerstraße 75, Dachau
🕐 9am–5pm daily ⬜ kz-gedenk staette-dachau.de ⬜
The first concentration camp was established in 1933 in Dachau (20 km/ 12 miles from Munich). Tours of the memorial site are available.

7. Kloster Wessobrunn
⬜ Klosterhof 4, Wessobrunn
⬜ kloster-wessobrunn.de ⬜
The stuccowork at this monastery, built in the 9th century, is renowned internationally. Only certain parts of the monastery are open to the public.

8. Murnauer Moos
⬜ murnau.de
A boardwalk leads into Bavaria's largest continuous moorland, spanning 32 sq km (12 sq miles).

9. Kochelsee and Walchensee
The Kochelsee and the Walchensee further south are perfect for wind-surfing. The Walchensee is the largest and deepest mountain lake in Germany (covering 16 sq km/6 sq miles, and up to 192 m/630 ft deep).

10. Oberammergau
This health resort, with Lüftlmalerei frescos, is world-famous for its *Passionsspiele* (staging of Jesus's passion), held every 10 years. The next ones are scheduled for 2032.

**Hiking on a trail in the
Murnauer Moos**

Places to Eat

PRICE CATEGORIES

Price of a three-course meal (or similar)
for one, with a glass of wine or beer,
including taxes and service.

€ below €30 €€ €30–60 €€€ over €60

1. Alpenhof Murnau

🏠 Ramsachstraße 8, Murnau
🌐 alpenhof-murnau.com · €€
Upscale Bavarian restaurant with
a panoramic view of the Alps.

2. Gletscherrestaurant Sonnalpin

🌐 zugspitze.de · €€
This restaurant on the Zugspitzplatt
glacial plateau is, at 2,600 m (8,530 ft),
the highest restaurant in Germany.

3. Klosterhotel Ettal

🏠 Kaiser-Ludwig-Platz 10–12, Ettal
🌐 klosterhotel-ettal.de · €€
Located near Ettal Abbey, a
Benedictine monastery, this
restaurant serves Bavarian cuisine.

4. Inselhotel zur Linde

🏠 Fraueninsel im Chiemsee
🌐 linde-frauenchiemsee.de · €€
This traditional, 600-year-old
hotel serves homemade cakes
and Bavarian specialities.

5. Gasthof zum Rassen

🏠 Ludwigstraße 45, Garmisch-
Partenkirchen 🌐 gasthof-zum-
rassen.inn.fan · €
A traditional inn, Gasthof zum Rassen
serves classic Bavarian fare and is
home to Germany's oldest folk theatre.

6. Midgardhaus

🏠 Midgardstraße 3–5, Tutzing 🕐 Mon
🌐 midgardhaus.de · €€
Serving top-notch breakfast through
to dinner on the terrace overlooking
Starnberg See, in the beer garden, or in
the conservatory of Midgard-Haus.

Murals adorning the Gasthof
zum Rassen

7. Seerestaurant Alpenblick

🏠 Kirchtalstraße 30, Uffing 🕐 Mon & Tue
🌐 seerestaurant-alpenblick.de · €€
The view of the Staffelsee from the
terrace and beer garden is sensational.
Great, seasonal food.

8. Hotel Alte Post

🏠 Dorfstraße 19, Oberammergau
🌐 altepost.com · €
Set in the town centre, this restaurant
serves Bavarian delicacies.

9. Herzogliches Bräustüberl Tegernsee

🏠 Schlossplatz 1, Tegernsee
🌐 braustuberl.de · €
A cosy and rustic Bavarian inn
with a lovely terrace.

10. Kreut-Alm

🏠 Kreut 1, Großweil 🌐 kreutalm.de · €
This restaurant offers a breathtaking
panoramic view of the mountains. It
also has a terrace and beer garden.

STREETSMART

Woman cycling in Hofgarten

GETTING AROUND

Whether exploring Munich on foot or making use of public transport, here is everything you need to know to navigate the city and the areas beyond the centre like a pro.

AT A GLANCE

PUBLIC TRANSPORT COSTS

U-BAHN

€3.90

Single journey
within one zone

DAY TICKET

€9.20

Zone M

ISARCARD
WEEKLY TICKET

€21.10

Zone M

SPEED LIMIT

REGIONAL
ROADS

100
km/h
(60 mph)

RURAL ROADS

70
km/h
(43 mph)

MOTORWAY

130
km/h
(80 mph)

URBAN
AREAS

50
km/h
(30 mph)

Arriving by Air

Munich Airport is a major hub for air travel, with many international and domestic airlines passing through. There are shops, restaurants and cafés, and a tourist information centre in the airport. Terminals 1 and 2 house the offices of over 100 airlines.
Munich Airport
Ⓦ munich-airport.de

International Train Travel

Regular high-speed international trains connect Germany to various towns and cities in Italy, Austria, France and Eastern Europe. **München Hauptbahnhof** (the city's central station) handles trains to and from Munich. In most cases, there are direct connections to major European cities several times a day. Southern Bavaria is very well connected thanks to its dense rail network.

You can buy tickets and passes for multiple international journeys via **Eurail** or **Interrail**; however, you may still need to pay an additional reservation fee depending on which rail service you travel with. Always check that your pass is valid before boarding.
Eurorail
Ⓦ eurail.com
Interrail
Ⓦ interrail.eu
München Hauptbahnhof
Ⓦ bahnhof.de/muenchen-hbf

Regional and Local Trains

Most German trains and railway lines are operated by **Deutsche Bahn AG**. Long-distance routes are served by InterCity Express (ICE), InterCity (IC) and EuroCity (EC) trains, while the network also runs Regional-Express (RE) and RegionalBahn (RB) for shorter distances.

The S-Bahn suburban trains cover a radius of 30–40 km (19–25 miles) around Munich and are ideal for taking day trips to the lakes or to Dachau. The S-Bahn is also an important means of transport within the city centre; its central stretch (11 km / 7 miles with all seven lines) between Donnersberger-brücke and Ostbahnhof offers connection points to the U-Bahn, buses and trams. During the week, S-Bahn trains run from 4:15am to 1am, every 10 to 20 minutes. On Fridays, Saturdays and some public holidays trains run all night. The majority of S-Bahn stations are wheelchair-accessible.

Deutsche Bahn AG
🆆 bahn.de

Long-Distance Bus Travel

Many long-distance buses arrive at and depart from the central bus terminal – **Zentraler Omnibusbahnhof (ZOB)** – at the Hackerbrücke. Tourist hotspots in Upper Bavaria are well served by a network of bus routes managed by the **Regionalverkehr Oberbayern**. Flixbus offers low-cost intercity travel in Europe.

FlixBus
🆆 flixbus.de
Regionalverkehr Oberbayern
🆆 rvo-bus.de
Zentraler Omnibusbahnhof (ZOB)
🆆 muenchen-zob.de

Public Transport

The **MVG** (Munich Transportation Corporation) and the **MVV** (Munich Traffic and Tariff Association) operate the city's public transport network. Timetables, transport maps, ticket information and mobility services can be obtained from customer service counters in München Hauptbahnhof, **Ostbahnhof** (Munich East train station) and Marienplatz. The MVG and MVV websites also feature a wealth of information, as well as interactive journey planners.

MVG
🆆 mvg.de
MVV
🆆 mvv-muenchen.de
Ostbahnhof
🆆 bahnhof.de/en/muenchen-ost

Tickets

All public transport operated by the MVG and the MVV uses the same tickets. These can be bought at ticket machines in U-Bahn and S-Bahn stations, on trams and buses or online as a mobile ticket. Several ticket types are available: multi-ride (Streifenkarten), single-ride (Einzelkarten), daily passes (Tageskarten), "IsarCard" weekly passes (Wochenkarten) and monthly passes (Monatskarten). Multi-ride tickets have to be validated for each zone (Munich has 12 zones with zone M covering the city centre). Visitors can take advantage of special rates with city discount cards (p145), which can be purchased from ticket machines, tourist centres or online.

U-Bahn

The U-Bahn underground rail network runs modern trains around the city. Nearly all of its stations, marked with a capital "U" on a blue background, are wheelchair-accessible. Eight lines are currently in operation within the city zone (the U8 is only intended as a booster line). In total, the network spans over 100 km (62 miles) and comprises over 100 stations. Like the S-Bahn train network, U-Bahn trains run from 4:15am to 1am daily and arrive every 5 to 10 minutes. On Fridays and Saturdays, and during some public holidays, U-Bahn trains run all through the night.

GETTING TO AND FROM THE AIRPORT			
Airport	**Transport**	**Journey Time**	**Price**
Munich Airport	S-Bahn (S1 and S8)	40 mins	€11.60
	Lufthansa Bus	45 mins	€10.50
	Airport Messe München Shuttle	45 mins	€11
	Taxi	45 mins	€60

Trams

Munich's tram network dates from 1876, when horsecars were used to transport locals around the city. Today, the network comprises 13 daytime and 4 night electric tram lines. The day lines operate from 4:45am to 1:30am, while the night lines operate from 1:30am to 4:30am daily. Most tram cars have ramps to allow wheelchair access.

Buses

Munich has an extensive bus network that covers most corners of the city and connects travellers to S-Bahn and U-Bahn services. Most buses operate from 5am to 1am, departing every 10 to 20 minutes. Night buses, recognizable from the "N" in front of the line number, operate throughout the night. Buses are usually equipped with air conditioning as well as low floors and ramps for wheelchair users.

Taxis

You can book a taxi by telephone, hail one or join a queue at a taxi rank. Official taxis in Munich are cream-coloured and have a TAXI sign on the roof. The minimum charge is €5.70, then €2.50 per km. Taxi services in the city include **Taxi München eG**, **Isar-Funk** and **Taxi Zentrale Freising**. Uber also operates in Munich.

IsarFunk
w isarfunk.de
Taxi München eG
w taxi-muenchen.com
Taxi Zentrale Freising
w taxifreising3661.de

Driving

Driving in Munich is possible but is generally no quicker than taking public transport. The centre is largely pedestrianized and parking is not only difficult but sometimes expensive.

Driving to Munich

Motorways and regional roads in Germany are well maintained and easy to navigate. Six motorways lead into Munich: the A8 Stuttgart/Salzburg, A95 Garmisch-Partenkirchen, A9 Nuremberg-Berlin, A92 Deggendorf, A96 Lindau, and A94 Passau. The Autobahnring ring road (A99, incomplete) lets you bypass the city in part. If you plan to drive into the city, you will need to take two additional ring roads: the Mittlerer Ring and, once you reach the centre, the Altstadtring.

Driving licences issued by any of the European Union member states are valid in the EU. If visiting from outside the EU, you may need to apply for an International Driving Permit. Always check with your local automobile association before you travel.

Driving in Munich

In 2008, Munich, like many other cities in Germany, introduced an **Environmental Green Zone** (Umweltzone). This only allows vehicles with an *Umweltplakette* (environmental badge) access to the zone, which encompasses the city centre. You will need to obtain this permit prior to travelling here by car. It can be bought online or from any participating garage in Germany.
Environment Green Zone
w green-zones.eu

Car Hire

Hire firms can be found at Munich airport and at the city's main railway stations. Popular companies such as **Hertz**, **Avis**, **Sixt** and **Budget** all have bases in Munich. In order to rent a car, drivers need to produce their passport, driving licence and a credit card with enough capacity to cover the excess.

Most rental agencies require drivers to be over the age of 21 and to have an international licence.
Avis
w avis.co.uk
Budget
w budget.co.uk
Hertz
w hertz.co.uk
Sixt
w sixt.co.uk

Parking

One of the biggest challenges for drivers is finding parking. Although there are many multi-storey car parks (*Park-Häus*), they are expensive and often full ("*frei*" indicates that spaces are available). Most hotels have some form of parking on offer, but this can come at an additional cost. The majority of on-street parking must be paid for, either by inserting coins into a meter or by buying a pay-and-display ticket. One hour is often the maximum in the centre and attendants issue fines when cars are illegally parked or parking is unpaid. Cars can be towed; retrieving them can be expensive and difficult.

Rules of the Road

Drive on the right. Unless otherwise signposted, vehicles coming from the right have priority.

At all times, drivers must carry a valid driver's licence, registration and insurance documents. The wearing of seat belts is compulsory for drivers and passengers. Lights must be used in tunnels and the use of a mobile phone while driving is prohibited, with the exception of a hands-free system.

All drivers must have third-party insurance (*Haftpflichtversicherung*) – it is the minimum insurance requirement in Germany. Drivers will be fined for speeding, tailgating and for parking offences. The drink-drive limit (*p145*) is strictly enforced. If you are drinking alcohol, use public transport or a taxi.

In case of breakdown, contact **ADAC** (German motoring club) for assistance; club members get discounted rates.

ADAC
C (089) 222222

Cycling

Munich is a bicycle-friendly city with plenty of cycle paths. The city centre is largely flat and easy to navigate, with cycle lanes marked on pavements and on the edges of roads. Bicycle stands are situated throughout the city, including facilities at railway and S-Bahn stations.

Bicycles can be taken on the U-Bahn and S-Bahn in the carriage marked with a cycle logo, except at rush hour from 6am to 9am and 4pm to 6pm. In addition to a passenger ticket, you will need to buy a one-day Farrad-Tageskarte for €2.60. You cannot take bikes on trams or buses, unless it is a fold-up bike.

The many bike-rental options include the **MVG Rad** system, which provides 1,200 bicycles across 125 stations, the **Call a Bike** system and **Pedalhelden**.

Cycling in Germany is subject to strict rules: these include speed limits, children under 8 not being allowed to use bike lanes, and cyclists needing to follow traffic lights. Like drivers, cyclists must travel on the right. If in doubt, dismount: many novices cross busy junctions on foot; if you do so, switch to the pedestrian section of the crossing. Wearing a helmet is recommended when cycling in the city, but it is not a legal requirement in Germany. Drink-drive limits here also apply to cyclists.

Call a Bike
W callabike-interaktiv.de
MVG Rad
W mvg.de
Pedalhelden
W pedalhelden.de

Walking

The best way to explore Munich is on foot. Much of the Old Town has been closed to traffic and many of the main tourist attractions are within a 20-minute walk of one another.

Visitors can escape the urban bustle with a walk through one of Munich's many parks. In summer, paths along the Isar River lead through lush greenery to beaches filled with sunbathers.

The Bavarian Alps promise lovely walks with numerous well-marked paths. The foothills of the Alps provide some easy terrain for gentle hikes, but the higher you go the more demanding it becomes. Ensure you have suitable boots, waterproof clothing, a map and a compass. Tell someone where you're going and when you plan to return.

PRACTICAL INFORMATION

A little local know-how goes a long way in Munich. On these pages you can find all the essential advice and information you will need to make the most of your trip.

AT A GLANCE

CURRENCY
Euro (EUR)

AVERAGE DAILY SPEND

SAVE	SPEND	SPLURGE
€60	**€125**	**€200+**

BOTTLED WATER	COFFEE	BEER	DINNER FOR TWO
€1.70	**€3.50**	**€4.00**	**€60**

ESSENTIAL PHRASES

Hello	Guten Tag (Grüss Gott in Bavaria)
Goodbye	Auf Wiedersehen
Please	Bitte
Thank you	Danke
Do you speak English?	Sprechen Sie Englisch?
I don't understand...	Ich verstehe nicht

ELECTRICITY SUPPLY
Power sockets are type C and F, both fitting two-pronged plugs. Standard voltage is 230 volts.

Passports and Visas
For entry requirements, including visas, consult your nearest German embassy or check the **German Federal Foreign Office** website. Citizens of the UK, US, Canada, Australia and New Zealand do not need visas for stays of up to three months but in future must apply in advance for the European Travel Information and Authorization System (**ETIAS**); roll-out has continually been postponed so check the website for details. EU nationals do not need a visa or an ETIAS.

ETIAS
Ⓦ travel-europe.europa.eu/etias_en
German Federal Foreign Office
Ⓦ auswaertiges-amt.de

Government Advice
Now more than ever, it is important to consult both your and the German government's advice before travelling. The UK Foreign, Commonwealth and Development Office (**FCDO**), the **US State Department**, the **Australian Department of Foreign Affairs and Trade** and the German Federal Foreign Office offer the latest information on security, health and local regulations.

Australian Department of Foreign Affairs and Trade
Ⓦ smartraveller.gov.au
UK FCDO
Ⓦ gov.uk/foreign-travel-advice
US State Department
Ⓦ travel.state.gov

Customs Information
You can find information on the laws relating to goods and currency taken in or out of Germany on the Federal Customs Service (**Zoll**) website.
Zoll
Ⓦ zoll.de

Insurance
We strongly recommend taking out a comprehensive insurance policy covering theft, loss of belongings,

medical care, cancellations and delays, and read the small print carefully.

UK citizens are eligible for free emergency medical care in Germany provided they have a valid European Health Insurance Card (EHIC) or UK Global Health Insurance Card (**GHIC**).

GHIC
🅦 ghic.org.uk

Vaccinations

There are no legal immunization requirements for visiting Germany. You may wish to be vaccinated against tick-borne encephalitis if you are planning to spend time in Bavaria's mountains or forested areas.

Money

Most establishments accept major credit, debit and prepaid currency cards. Contactless payments have become the norm in recent years, though they are still not generally used on public transport. It is always worth carrying cash, as some smaller restaurants and beer gardens don't accept card.

Cash machines (ATMs) can be found everywhere. It is customary to tip between 5 per cent and 10 per cent, and when buying a beer at a bar, to round up to the nearest euro.

Travellers with Specific Requirements

Germany is ahead of the curve when it comes to barrier-free travel. Most S-Bahn and U-Bahn stations are accessible for those with specific requirements while buses and trams cater to travellers using wheelchairs, and passengers can inform the driver of their destination, who will assist if necessary. Special city tours for those who require specific adjustments are run by the city's tourism website, **Simply Munich**. The site also provides a list of venues that have special access.

The **Club Behinderter und ihrer Freunde** (Club for the Disabled and Friends, or CBF) provides information on accessible cinemas, theatres and museums. It also organizes events and offers support for cultural events. Additional advice and information about wheelchair rentals is also available online from **VDK Bayern**.

Visitors should be aware that several areas in the city have original cobble-stone paving, which may prove difficult to traverse for wheelchair users. Similarly, some restaurants in old buildings may have limited access. It's always worth checking ahead.

Club Behinderter und ihrer Freunde
🅦 cbf-muenchen.de
Simply Munich
🅦 muenchen-tourismus-barrierefrei.de
VDK Bayern
🅦 vdk.de

Language

German is the official language in Munich, but English is widely spoken throughout the city. You can generally get by knowing minimal German, but a few niceties in the local language are usually appreciated. English is less commonly spoken outside the city centre and in the Bavarian Alps.

Opening Hours

Most shops in the city centre are open Monday to Saturday, 9am to 8pm and are closed on Sundays. Offices, banks and post offices tend to close earlier, usually by 4, 5 or 6pm, and remain closed on Sundays. A number of city museums charge €1 on Sunday. Some museums, attractions and restaurants close for the day on Monday.

Public transport services are reduced on Sundays.

On public holidays, most post offices, shops, banks and some attractions, close for the day.

Situations can change quickly and unexpectedly. Always check before visiting attractions and hospitality venues for up-to-date opening hours and booking requirements.

Personal Security

Munich has one of the lowest crime rates in Europe. However, pickpockets still operate in busy tourist areas and on public transport. Use your common sense and either leave valuables in a hotel safe or keep them out of sight. Take extra care during Oktoberfest.

AT A GLANCE

EMERGENCY NUMBERS

GENERAL EMERGENCY	AMBULANCE
112	**112**

FIRE SERVICE	POLICE
112	**110**

TIME ZONE
CET/CEST
Central European Summer Time runs from late March to late October.

TAP WATER
Unless otherwise stated, tap water in Germany is safe to drink.

WEBSITES AND APPS

Simply Munich
The city's official tourist information website (www.munich.travel).
MVGO
This public transport app includes a journey planner and live departures.
story2go München
An audio guide app that takes visitors on tours of the city.
www.bavaria.travel
Bavaria's official tourism website.

If you have anything stolen, report the crime as soon as possible to the nearest police station. Get a copy of the crime report in order to claim on your insurance. Contact your embassy if you have your passport stolen, or in the event of a serious crime or accident.

Germans are generally accepting of all people, regardless of their race, gender or sexuality. The country legalized homosexuality in 1994 and same-sex marriage has been legal since 2017. Despite this, acceptance is not always a given and If you do feel unsafe at any time, the **Safe Space Alliance** pinpoints your nearest place of refuge. **Diversity** runs a youth centre and café offering support to the LGBTQ+ community. Further help can be found through **Sub**, a support association for gay men, and **LeTRa**, which provides counselling at its community centre for lesbians.
Diversity
diversity-muenchen.de
LeTRa
letra.de/en
Safe Space Alliance
safespacealliance.com
Sub
subonline.org

Health

Germany has a world-class health service with excellent hospitals and clinics with emergency departments. EU citizens are eligible to receive emergency medical treatment in Germany free of charge. If you have an EHIC or GHIC (p143), present this as soon as possible. For visitors from outside the EU, payment of medical expenses is the patient's responsibility. It is important to arrange comprehensive medical insurance before travel.

Chemists (Apotheke) are easy to spot with their red "A", and are usually open 8am–6pm. Details of the nearest 24-hour service are posted in all pharmacy windows or can be found online through the **emergency service portal**.
Emergency Service Portal
lak-bayernnotdienst-portal.de

Smoking, Alcohol and Drugs

Germany has a smoking ban in all public places, including bars, restaurants and hotels. Some establishments circumvent these laws by calling themselves a *Raucher-Kneipe*, or smoking pub.

The possession of narcotics is prohibited and could result in prosecution and a prison sentence.

Unless stated otherwise, it is permitted to drink alcohol on the streets and in public parks and gardens. Germany has a strict limit of 0.05 per cent BAC (blood alcohol content) for drivers.

ID

There is no requirement for visitors to carry ID, but you may be asked to show your passport. If you don't have it with you, the police may escort you to wherever your passport is being kept.

Responsible Travel

Munich has been at the forefront of sustainable travel since the end of World War II and there are many ways to travel responsibly today. Visitors can do their bit by utilizing the city's excellent public transport system or by walking and cycling if you're able to do so.

Munich also has a reusable culture and many cafés will allow you to use your own coffee cup. Moreover, water refill points are growing in number with many around Viktualienmarkt. If you do purchase a bottled drink, the "Pfand" scheme means you can return the empty bottle to shops selling that drink to get your money refunded.

The **Simply Munich** website has information and suggestions on how to make your trip more sustainable.
Simply Munich
w munich.travel/en

Local Customs

Germany has strict laws on hate speech and symbols linked to the Nazis. Disrespectful behaviour can warrant a fine, or prosecution. Pay attention to signs indicating when photos aren't allowed and think about how you compose any shots.

Mobile Phones and Wi-Fi

Phone coverage is generally good and phones can even be used on the U-Bahn without any issues. Visitors travelling to Germany with EU tariffs can use their mobile phones abroad without being affected by data-roaming charges. Visitors from other countries should check their contracts before using their phone in Germany in order to avoid unexpected charges.

High-speed internet and Wi-Fi is available in cafés and hotels, and many tourist areas also have free Wi-Fi hotspots. A list of free **Wi-Fi hotspots** can be found on the city's website.
Wi-Fi Hotspots
w muenchen.de

Postal Services

German post offices and post boxes are easy to spot with their distinctive yellow Deutsche Post signs. Stamps (*Briefmarken*) can be bought in post offices, newsagents, tobacconists and most major supermarkets.

Taxes and Refunds

VAT is 19 per cent in Germany. Non-EU residents are entitled to a tax refund subject to certain conditions. You must request a tax receipt and export papers (*Ausfuhrbescheinigung*) when you purchase your goods. When leaving the country, present these papers, along with the receipt and your ID, at customs to receive your refund.

Discount Cards

The **Munich Card** and **Munich City Pass** offer free or discounted entry to many attractions throughout the city, including museums, galleries, tours and selected restaurants. They also cover the cost of public transport for the duration of the card's use, which ranges from 24 hours to 5 days.
Munich Card
w mvv-muenchen.de/en
Munich City Pass
w munich.travel/en/offers/booking/munich-city-pass

PLACES TO STAY

From ultra-modern hotels to traditional Bavarian guest houses, Munich has accommodation for every traveller. Stay in the Old Town to experience the city buzz or soak up Munich's history in the Museum District. Adventurous holidaygoers can look further afield for comfortable options near the Alps.

   Hotels fill up quickly and prices rise around Christmas, Oktoberfest and during the summer, so book ahead when possible. There is no tourist tax but Wi-Fi and breakfast may be an additional cost.

> **PRICE CATEGORIES**
> For a standard double room per night (with breakfast if included), taxes and extra charges.
> ....
> € under €130
> €€ €130–€270
> €€€ over 270

Southern Old Town

Platzl Hotel

📍 N3 🏠 Sparkassenstraße 10 🌐 platzl.de · €€€

Nestled in the heart of the Old Town, this hotel might have the best location in Munich. The iconic Hofbräuhaus beer hall is just next door and the Marienplatz around the corner, so you can easily spend your days exploring – but make sure to return in the evenings for dinner in the on-site Pfistermühle restaurant, set in the vaults of a 16th-century mill.

Hotel Königshof

📍 L3 🏠 Karlsplatz 25 🌐 marriott.com/en-gb/hotels/muclh-hoenigshof-a-luxury-collection-hotel-munich · €€€

The starkly modern exterior of this hotel may be divisive in its neighbourhood of preserved historical buildings, but you won't mind once inside. The rooms are beautifully designed with a curated selection of local art and feature cutting-edge technology, giving each a sense of modern luxury. Best of all, the hotel has one of the city's premier restaurants, GRETA OTO, serving up sumptuous South American dishes.

BEYOND by Geisel

📍 N4 🏠 Marienplatz 22 🌐 beyond-muc.de · €€

This boutique hotel is like a home away from home, albeit a very luxurious one. Sink into a comfy chair with a book from the library-cum-lobby, watch the hotel chefs at work in the kitchen (they'll whip you up a meal on request) and pair your meal with a bottle of wine from the wine lounge – just like home, right?

Falkenturm Boutique Hotel

📍 N3 🏠 Falkenturmstraße 3 🌐 hotel-falkenturm.de · €€€

Just off Munich's bustling luxury shopping street Maximilianstraße, is this charming boutique hotel. Though the rooms are compact, they are spacious enough for comfy beds and are one of the few Munich hotels with air conditioning – an essential in the summertime. The hotel is perfect for quiet respite after a busy day spent out and about in town.

Northern Old Town

Bayerischer Hof

📍 M3 🏠 Promenadepl 2-6 🌐 bayerischerhof.de · €€€

What do The Beatles, Muhammad Ali and Sophia Loren have in common? They've all stayed in the historic rooms of this Munich institution. Open since 1841, the hotel remains a city icon thanks to its regal rooms, luxurious facilities and superb restaurants, which include the world-class two-Michelin-starred Atelier.

Unsölds Factory Hotel

📍 P3 🏠 Unsöldstraße 10 🌐 unsoelds-hotel.de · €€

This hotel is a great base from which to explore Munich's central sights. Immediately to the south is the Old Town, to the west is the grandiose Residenz and just to the north is the Englischer Garten. Whether you want to spend your days taking in the sights or relaxing in abundant greenery, Unsölds is the perfect starting point.

Hotel Vier Jahreszeiten Kempinski München

⑨ N3 **⌂** Maximilianstraße 17 **ⓦ** hempinshi.com/en/hotel-vier-jahreszeiten · €€€

Immerse yourself in Bavarian luxury at this historic Munich hotel. First opened in 1858, it has hosted empresses, archdukes and queens – so you can expect the royal treatment. The hotel offers a private butler service, limousine hire and a traditional British-style afternoon tea, all within a lavish building that retains its original period features.

Museum Quarter

Ruby Lilly

⑨ E4 **⌂** Dachauer Str. 37 **ⓦ** ruby-hotels.com · €

A few nights at Ruby Lilly and you're sure to feel like a rockstar. This funky music-themed hotel has a Marshall speaker in each room and guitars hanging from the walls of the bar, where guests are encouraged to sing and perform their hearts out. Rehearse in your room before borrowing one of the guitars and

taking to the stage. And don't worry about your neighbours – the rooms are soundproof.

The Charles Hotel

⑨ L2 **⌂** Sophienstraße 28 **ⓦ** roccofortehotels.com · €€€

After a stay at the Charles Hotel you might feel like you've spent more time outside than in. This luxury hotel is a green oasis in the already leafy Lenbach Gärten district. Inspiration drawn from its green surroundings is visible in every corner of the hotel, from the soft earthy furnishings found throughout to the botanically themed cocktails.

KING's HOTEL First Munich

⑨ L2 **⌂** Dachauer Str. 13 **ⓦ** hingshotels.de/en/first-hotel-munich · €

This traditional hotel is adored for many reasons: an excellent location, gorgeous wood canopy beds and stunning art in gilded frames that adorn the lobby and corridors. It is a particular favourite among business travellers and digital nomads for its dedicated Focus Lounge coworking space.

Hotel Erzgiesserei

⑨ E3 **⌂** Erzgießereistraße 15 **ⓦ** europe-hotels-international.de · €€

Just to the west of the Museum District, the Erzgiesserei is perfectly located to be far enough away from the noisy

centre to ensure a good night's sleep but still close enough to walk to the major sights upon waking. Art and history lovers will appreciate that the three Pinakothek galleries and the Museum Brandhorst are just a few minutes' stroll away.

Schwabing and the University Quarter

ANDAZ Munich Schwabinger Tor

⑨ G1 **⌂** Leopoldstraße 170 **ⓦ** hyatt.com/andaz · €€€

With its five distinct restaurants and bars, no one goes hungry at Andaz Munich. Start your day with a coffee and homemade pastry at Bicicletta and end your evening with a cocktail at the Lounge Bar and a meal of world-class cellar-aged steak at the hotel's Lonely Broccoli restaurant.

Flemings Hotel München Schwabing

⑨ G2 **⌂** Leopoldstraße 130-132 **ⓦ** flemings-hotels.com/hotel-muenchen-schwabing · €

Few hotels offer better value for money than this bright hotel. With colourful vases and armchairs throughout the rooms and an Italian restaurant serving up delicious salads and desserts, each stay is a treat. End your day at the restaurant's outdoor terrace, the perfect spot for a sunset spritz.

HOtello Schwabing

⑨ F3 ⌂ Hohenzollern-straße 9 ⓦ hotello.de · €€

Looking for a peaceful getaway but still want to be close to the action? The HOtello Schwabing has you covered. This modern hotel is a peaceful sanctuary on a quiet side street in Schwabing, but it has great transport links to the centre of town, along with an underground car park.

Pension am Siegestor

⑨ F3 ⌂ Akademiestraße 5 ⓦ siegestor.de · €€

For unbeatable views of the University and Siegestor (Victory Gate), look no further than this traditional, family-run guesthouse. While it's not the most modern looking hotel in Munich, the staff are always kind and thoughtful and the city views alone are worth the price.

Schwabinger Wahrheit by Geisel

⑨ F3 ⌂ Hohenzollern-straße 5 ⓦ schwabinger-wahrheit.de · €€

Relaxation is an art form at this elegant hotel. The stylish wellness area has a Finnish sauna, outdoor jacuzzi with panoramic views and well-equipped gym. You can just as easily wind down in one of the comfortable and clean rooms, but for the ultimate luxury stay, you'll want to book suite 63: it comes complete with its own in-room sauna and bar.

Along the Isar

Flushing Meadows

⑨ F5 ⌂ Fraunhoferstraße 32 ⓦ flushingmeadows hotel.com · €€

This hip boutique hotel takes playful design to its extremes. The 11 suites were all designed by a variety of international creatives, including DJs, bartenders, actors, artists and even a surfer. With such a variety, it's hardly surprising that each room is completely unique. Expect lifesized skeletons, a floating bed and artwork from a wide range of genres and mediums.

JAMS Music Hotel

⑨ G5 ⌂ Stubenvollstraße 2 ⓦ jams-hotel.com · €€

This is the ultimate destination for music lovers. The lobby walls are covered with several hundred vinyl records for you to browse and bring back to your room to enjoy on your own record player, and each floor is dedicated to a specific music legend. For the musically inclined, JAMS hits all the right notes.

Marias Platzl

⑨ F6 ⌂ Mariahilfpl. 4 ⓦ mariasplatzl.de · €€

The little sibling of the famous Platzl hotel, the Marias was created to celebrate the traditions and craft skills of Munich. Walls feature wood panelling, traditional artworks and coverings made from Dirndl fabric, all produced by local

crafters – a stay here is an immersion in Munich's cultural history.

South West

Roomers Munich

⑨ D4 ⌂ Landsberger Str. 68 ⓦ roomers-hotels. com/en/munich · €€€

Few hotels are as stylish as the high-concept Roomers. The hotel has an ultra-modern Avant-Garde design complete with moody lighting. Its styling extends to the hotel's fantastic Japanese-inspired Izakaya Asian Kitchen & Bar, where you can have a front-row seat to the chef's action.

Hotel Krone

⑨ D5 ⌂ Theresienhöhe 8 ⓦ hotel-krone-muenchen. de · €€

Want to absorb the Oktoberfest energy? Look no further than Hotel Krone. It's located across the street from where the festival takes place and some rooms have balconies that overlook the grounds so you never miss a minute of the action. Even better, you won't have far to go after a long day sampling fine beers.

Hotel Mariandl

⑨ E5 ⌂ Goethestraße 51 ⓦ mariandl.com · €

Embrace the old-fashioned charms of the Hostal Mariandl. This beautiful belle-époque building retains many of its original features, including a mahogany bar, a well-worn oak staircase and stucco ceilings with chandeliers. It does not have TVs or a Wi-Fi, so prepare to truly step back into the past.

Motel One Munich Westend

◉ D4 ⌂ Landsberger Str. 79 🌐 motel-one.com · €€

Part of the Motel One chain, this hotel has everything you need for a cosy city break. Rooms are compact but well-appointed and communal areas feature furniture that showcases local design and craft; there are deep sofas and armchairs to sink into and enjoy your favourite holiday read.

North West

Hotel Motel One München-Olympia Gate

◉ E2 ⌂ Petra-Kelly-Straße 4 🌐 motel-one.com · €

This hotel embraces its spot next to Olympiapark with an all-out Olympic theme. Gold medals and graphic prints of athletes decorate the walls and the furniture transports you back to 1972. Families should note that kids under twelve stay for free when sharing a room with their parents, so embrace the whole-some fun as a family.

Leonardo Hotel Munich City Olympiapark

◉ D2 ⌂ Dachauer Str. 199 🌐 leonardo-hotels.com · €

This comfortable hotel is in a great location – close

to the Olympiapark and the unusual modern designs of the BMW Museum and BMW Welt. Simple yet stylish, there's an on-site bistro and optional breakfast add-on. Moreover, the hotel is one of the few Munich stays to include a secure and spacious under-ground car park, which has a number of charging points for electric cars.

Beyond Munich

Das Kranzbach

⌂ In Kranzbach 1 🌐 daskranzbach.de · €€€

Built in the style of an early 10th-century English country manor by an English aristocrat, Das Kranzbach sits some-what incongruously with its Bavarian surroundings. These days, it's a key fixture of local society and a hive for activity, ranging from hiking and biking to cross-country skiing and horse riding.

Obermühle

⌂ Mühlstraße 22 🌐 hotel-obermuehle.de · €€

This remarkable hotel has been family owned and operated since 1634, so expect a warm welcome that's been honed over nearly 400 years. It's an ideal base from which to embark upon adventures in the nearby Alps. Start your day with breakfast from the extensive buffet, then head on out: perhaps for a hike in summer or to ski in winter (rent skis from the front desk).

Abasto Hotel Dachau

⌂ Emmy-Noether Str. 4 🌐 abasto-dachau.de · €

This hotel, east of Dachau, has stunning views of the city. Within walking distance of both the Dachau Concentration Camp Memorial and Schloss Dachau, its location is primed for exploring the area's history. After a day of walking, enjoy a meal at the hotel's BRUSKO Grill restaurant.

Die Post Landgasthof Aufkirchen

⌂ Marienpl. 2 🌐 post-aufkirchen.de · €€

A traditional inn, Die Post delivers an idyllic rural stay in a hotel filled with locally made Bavarian furnishings. There are several dining halls, all decorated in traditional Bavarian style, and the peaceful beer garden is the perfect spot to relax with a drink after a long day.

Bussi Baby

⌂ Sanktjohanserstraße 46 🌐 bussibaby.com · €€€

Located close to the peaceful Tegernsee, Bussi Baby is a chic hotel known for its fabulous views over the Bavarian Alps. Make the most of its views with a trip to the relaxing rooftop spa or a dip in the rooftop infinity pool, best enjoyed while sipping on one of the signature cocktails from the hotel's Boom Boom bar.

INDEX

PHRASE BOOK

In an Emergency

Where is the telephone?	Wo ist das Telefon?	voh ist duss tel-e-fon?
Help!	Hilfe!	hilf-uh
Please call a doctor	Bitte rufen Sie einen Arzt	bitt-uh roof'n zee ine-en artst
Please call the police	Bitte rufen Sie die Polizei	bitt-uh roof'n zee dee poli-tsy
Please call the fire brigade	Bitte rufen Sie die Feuerwehr	bitt-uh roof'n zee dee foyer-vayr
Stop!	Halt!	hult

Communication Essentials

Yes	Ja	yah
No	Nein	nine
Please	Bitte	bitt-uh
Thank you	Danke	dunk-uh
Excuse me	Verzeihung	fair-tsy-hoong
Hello (good day)	Guten Tag	goot-en tahk
Hello	Grüß Gott	grooss got
Goodbye	Auf Wiedersehen	owf-veed-er-zay-em
Good evening	Guten Abend	goot'n ahb'nt
Good night	Gute Nacht	goot-uh nukht
Until tomorrow	Bis morgen	biss morg'n
See you	Tschüss	chooss
See you	Servus	sayr voos
What is that?	Was ist das?	voss ist duss
Why?	Warum?	var-room
Where?	Wo?	voh
When?	Wann?	vunn
today	heute	hoyt-uh
tomorrow	morgen	morg'n
month	Monat	mohn-aht
night	Nacht	nukht
afternoon	Nachmittag	nahkh-mit-tahk
morning	Morgen	morg'n
year	Jahr	yar
there	dort	dort
here	hier	hear
week	Woche	vokh-uh
yesterday	gestern	gest'n
evening	Abend	ahb'nt

Useful Phrases

How are you? (informal)	Wie geht's?	vee gayts
Fine, thanks	Danke, es geht mir gut	dunk-uh, es gayt meer goot
Until later	Bis später	biss shpay-ter
Where is/are..?	Wo ist/sind…?	voh ist/sind
How far is it to…?	Wie weit ist es…?	vee vite ist ess
Do you speak English?	Sprechen Sie Englisch?	shpresh'n zee eng-glish
I don't understand	Ich verstehe nicht	ish fair-shtay-uh nisht
Could you speak more slowly?	Könnten Sie langsamer sprechen?	kurnt'n zee lung-zam-er shpresh'n

Useful Words

large	groß	grohss
small	klein	kline
hot	heiß	hyce
cold	kalt	kult
good	gut	goot
bad	böse/schlecht	burss-uh/shlesht
open	geöffnet	g'urff-nett
closed	geschlossen	g'shloss'n
left	links	links
right	rechts	reshts
straight ahead	geradeaus	g'rah-der-owss

Making a Telephone Call

I would like to make a phone call	Ich möchte telefonieren	ish mer-shtuh tel-e-fon-eer'n
I'll try again later	Ich versuche es später noch einmal	ish fair-zookh-uh es shpay-ter nokh ine-mull
Can I leave a message?	Kann ich eine Nachricht hinterlassen?	kan ish ine-uh nakh-risht hint-er-lahss-en
answerphone	Anrufbeantworter	an-roof-be-ahnt-vort-er
telephone card	Telefonkarte	tel-e-fon-kart-uh
receiver	Hörer	hur-er
mobile	Handy	han-dee
engaged (busy)	besetzt	b'zetst
wrong number	falsche Verbindung	falsh-uh fair-bin-doong

Sightseeing

entrance ticket	Eintrittskarte	ine-tritz-kart-uh
cemetery	Friedhof	freed-hofe
train station	Bahnhof	barn-hofe
gallery	Galerie	gall-er-ree
information	Auskunft	owss-koonft
church	Kirche	keersh-uh
garden	Garten	gart'n
palace/castle	Palast/Schloss	pall-ast/shloss
place (square)	Platz	plats
bus stop	Haltestelle	hal-te-shtel-uh
theatre	Theater	tay-aht-er
free admission	Eintritt frei	ine-tritt fry

Shopping

Do you have/ Is there…?	Gibt es…?	geept ess
How much does it cost?	Was kostet das?	voss kost't duss?
When do you open/ close?	Wann öffnen Sie? schließen Sie?	vunn off'n zee shlees'n zee
this	das	duss
expensive	teuer	toy-er
cheap	preiswert	price-vurt
size	Größe	gruhs-ah
number	Nummer	noom-er
colour	Farbe	farb-uh
brown	braun	brown
black	schwarz	shvarts
red	rot	roht
blue	blau	blau
green	grün	groon
yellow	gelb	gelp

Types of Shop

chemist (pharmacy)	Apotheke	appo-tay-kuh
bank	Bank	bunk
market	Markt	markt
travel agency	Reisebüro	rye-zer-boo-roe
department store	Warenhaus	vahr'n-howss
chemist's, drugstore	Drogerie	droog-er-ree
hairdresser	Friseur	freezz-er
newspaper kiosk	Zeitungskiosk	tsytoongs-kee-osk
bookshop	Buchhandlung	bookh-hant-loong
bakery	Bäckerei	beck-er-eye
butcher	Metzgerei	mets-ger-eye
post office	Post	posst
shop/store	Geschäft/Laden	gush-eft/lard'n
clothes shop	Kleiderladen, Boutique	kly-der-lard'n boo-teek-uh

Staying in a Hotel

Do you have any vacancies?	Haben Sie noch Zimmer frei?	harb'n zee nokh tsimm-er-fry
with twin beds?	mit zwei Betten?	mitt tsvy bett'n
with a double bed?	mit einem Doppelbett?	mitt ine'm dopp'l-bet
with a bath?	mit Bad?	mitt bart
with a shower?	mit Dusche?	mitt doosh-uh
I have a reservation	Ich habe eine Reservierung	ish harb-uh ine-uh rez-er-veer-oong
key	Schlüssel	shlooss'l
porter	Pförtner	pfert-ner

Eating Out

Do you have a table for…?	Haben Sie einen Tisch für…?	harb'n zee tish foor
I would like to reserve a table	Ich möchte eine Reservierung machen	ish mer-shtuh ine-uh rezer-veer-oong makh'n
I'm a vegetarian	Ich bin Vegetarier	ish bin vegg-er-tah-ree-er
Waiter!	Herr Ober!	hair oh-bare!
The bill (check), please	Die Rechnung, bitte	dee resh-noong bitt-uh
breakfast	Frühstück	froo-shtock
lunch	Mittagessen	mit-targ-ess'n
dinner	Abendessen	arb'nt-ess'n
bottle	Flasche	flush-uh
dish of the day	Tagesgericht	tahg-es-gur-isht
main dish	Hauptgericht	howpt-gur-isht
dessert	Nachtisch	nahkh-tish
cup	Tasse	tass-uh
wine list	Weinkarte	vine-kart-uh
glass	Glas	glars
spoon	Löffel	lerff'l
fork	Gabel	gahb'l
teaspoon	Teelöffel	tay-lerff'l
knife	Messer	mess-er
starter (appetizer)	Vorspeise	for-shpize-uh
the bill	Rechnung	resh-noong
tip	Trinkgeld	trink-gelt
plate	Teller	tell-er

Menu Decoder

Apfel	upf'l	apple
Apfelsine	upf'l-seen-uh	orange
Aprikose	upri-kawz-uh	apricot
Artischocke	arti-shokh-uh-	artichoke
Aubergine	or-ber-jeen-uh	aubergine (eggplant)
Banane	bar-narn-uh	banana
Beefsteak	beef-stayk	steak
Bier	beer	beer
Bohnensuppe	burn-en-zoop-uh	bean soup
Bratkartoffeln	brat-kar-toff'l'n	fried potatoes
Bratwurst	brat-voorst	fried sausage
Brezel	bret-sell	pretzel
Brot	brot	bread
Brühe	bruh-uh	broth
Butter	boot-ter	butter
Champignon	shum-pin-yong	mushroom
Currywurst	kha-ree-voorst	sausage with curry sauce
Ei	eye	egg
Eis	ice	ice/ ice cream
Ente	ent-uh	duck
Erdbeeren	ayrt-beer'n	strawberries
Fisch	fish	fish
Fleisch	flysh	meat
Forelle	for-ell-uh	trout
Gans	ganns	goose
gebraten	g'braat'n	fried
Geflügel	g'floog'l	poultry
gegrillt	g'grilt	grilled
gekocht	g'kokht	boiled

Gemüse	g'mooz-uh	vegetables
geräuchert	g'rowk-ert	smoked
Gulasch	goo-lush	goulash
Hähnchen	haynsh'n	chicken
Hering	hair-ing	herring
Himbeeren	him-beer'n	raspberries
Kaffee	kaf-fay	coffee
Kalbfleisch	kalp-flysh	veal
Kaninchen	ka-neensh'n	rabbit
Karotte	car-ott-uh	carrot
Kartoffelpüree	kar-toff'l-poor-ay	mashed potatoes
Käse	kayz-uh	cheese
Knoblauch	k'nob-lowkh	garlic
Knödel	k'nerd'l	dumpling
Kuchen	kookh'n	cake
Lachs	lahkhs	salmon
Leber	lay-ber	liver
Marmelade	marmer-lard-uh	marmalade, jam
Milch	milsh	milk
Mineralwasser	minn-er-arl vuss-er	mineral water
Nuss	nooss	nut
Öl	erl	oil
Olive	o-leev-uh	olive
Pfeffer	pfeff-er	pepper
Pfirsch	pfir-sh	peach
Pflaume	pflow-me	plum
Pommes frites	pomm-fritt	chips/ French fries
Rindfleisch	rint-flysh	beef
Rührei	rhoo-er-eye	scrambled eggs
Saft	zuft	juice
Salat	zal-aat	salad
Salz	zults	salt
Sauerkirschen	zow-er-keersh'n	cherries
Sauerkraut	zow-er-krowt	sauerkraut
Sekt	zekt	sparkling wine
Senf	zenf	mustard
scharf	sharf	spicy
Schnitzel	shnitz'l	veal or pork cutlet
Schweinefleisch	shvine-flysh	pork
Semmel	tsem-mel	bread roll
Spargel	shparg'l	asparagus
Spiegelei	shpeeg'l-eye	fried egg
Spinat	shpin-art	spinach
Tee	tay	tea
Tomate	tom-art-uh	tomato
Wein	vine	wine
Weintrauben	vine-trowb'n	grapes
Wiener Würstchen	veen-er voorst-sh'n	frankfurter
Zitrone	tsi-trohn-uh	lemon
Zucker	tsook-er	sugar
Zwiebel	tsveeb'l	onion

Numbers

0	null	nool
1	eins	eye'ns
2	zwei	tsvy
3	drei	dry
4	vier	feer
5	fünf	foonf
6	sechs	zex
7	sieben	zeeb'n
8	acht	uhkht
9	neun	noyn
10	zehn	tsayn
11	elf	elf
12	zwölf	tsverlf
13	dreizehn	dry-tsayn
14	vierzehn	feer-tsayn
15	fünfzehn	foonf-tsayn
16	sechzehn	zex-tsayn
17	siebzehn	zeep-tsayn
18	achtzehn	uhkht-tsayn
19	neunzehn	noyn-tsayn
20	zwanzig	tsvunn-tsig

ACKNOWLEDGMENTS

This edition updated by

Contributor Rachel Preece

Senior Editors Dipika Dasgupta, Alison McGill

Senior Designers Laura O'Brien, Vinita Venugopal

Project Editors Charlie Baker, Anuroop Sanwalia

Assistant Editor Anjasi N. N.

Assistant Art Editor Amisha Gupta

Proofreader Clare Rudd-Jones

Indexer Gina Guilinger

Picture Research Deputy Manager Virien Chopra

Picture Research Team Nishwan Rasool, Samrajkumar S

Publishing Assistant Simona Velikova

Jacket Designers Laura O'Brien, Vinita Venugopal

Jacket Picture Researcher Laura O'Brien

Senior Cartographers Subhashree Bharati James Macdonald

Cartography Manager Suresh Kumar

Senior DTP Designer Tanveer Zaidi

DTP Designers Rohit Rojal, Ashok Kumar, Jagtar Singh

Pre-production Manager Balwant Singh

Image Retouching-Production Manager Pankaj Sharma

Production Controller Kariss Ainsworth

Managing Editors Beverly Smart, Hollie Teague

Managing Art Editor Gemma Doyle

Senior Managing Art Editor Priyanka Thakur

Art Director Maxine Pedliham

Publishing Director Georgina Dee

DK would like to thank the following for their contribution to the previous editions: Andiamo! Language Services, Hilary Bird, Marc di Duca, Dr Elfi Ledig, Clare Peel, Lisa Zammit.

The publisher would like to thank the following for their kind permission to reproduce their photographs:

(Key: a-above; b-below/bottom; c-centre; f-far; l-left; r-right; t-top)

123RF.com: Foottoo 12br, 14.

Alamy Stock Photo: Album 8, Ancient Art and Architecture 9tl, B.O'Kane 15tr, Manfred Bail 52t, Norman Barrett 44cla, Menigault Bernard 39b, CBW 28crb, Sunny Celeste 9cra, Chromorange / Ralph Peters 69t, Ian Dagnall 38b, 39t, Ian G Dagnall 29, Danita Delimont / Walter Bibikow 91, Digital-Fotofusion Gallery 137, DPA Picture Alliance 98t, DPA Picture Alliance / Angelika Warmuth 110t, DPA Picture Alliance / Felix Hörhager 127t, DPA Picture Alliance / Peter Kneffel 42b, 61t, 62, Glasshouse Images / Circa Images 10br, Manfred Glueck 53t, Dennis Hallinan 95t, Hemis / Mattes Ren 13cla, Hemis.fr / Planchard Eric 28br, Johann Hinrichs 80, 102, Icp / Incamerastock 28cb, Image Professionals GmbH / Franz Marc Frei 129b, Image Professionals GmbH / LOOK-foto 56–57bc, 134b, Image Professionals GmbH / Thomas Stankiewicz 104, imageBROKER com GmbH & Co. KG / Guenter Graefenhain 27t, 33b, imageBROKER.com GmbH & Co. KG / MAL 48b, imageBROKER.com GmbH & Co. KG / Manfred Bail 28bl, 58, 72b, 81b, 90, 96, 98b, 101b, 106, 117t, imageBROKER.com GmbH & Co. KG / Martin Siepmann 51t, imageBROKER.com GmbH & Co. KG / Moritz Wolf 5, 50–51b, 112b, 128b, Imago 12cr, Imago / Stefan M. Prager 75t, Imago / Wolfgang Maria Weber 64, 83, Interfoto / Fine Arts 27b, 102tl, Interfoto / History 31tl, Interfoto / Personalities 9cr, Jayskyland Images 128t, Engin Korkmaz 119b, Art Kowalsky 79b, Luis Emilio Villegas Amador 25bl, mauritius images GmbH / Franziska Maier 135t, mauritius images GmbH / Josefine Clasen 59b, nagelestock.com 134t, Old Paper Studios 9br, Werner Otto 13tl, Panther Media GmbH / Spitzi-Foto 37b, PjrWindows 25cb, Prisma Archivo 21c, Realworldmoments 105, Realy Easy Star 10tl, Matthias Riedinger 66t, Riccardo Sala 20c, Maurice Savage 49, 92, Süddeutsche Zeitung Photo / Catherina Hess 115, Süddeutsche Zeitung Photo / Claus Schunk 57t, Süddeutsche Zeitung Photo / Horstmüller 10clb, Süddeutsche Zeitung Photo / Stephan Rumpf 70–71bc, Sueddeutsche Zeitung Photo / Robert Haas 121, Sueddeutsche Zeitung Photo / Scherl 10cl, Sueddeutsche Zeitung Photo / Stephan Rumpf 73b, Westend61 GmbH 109t.

Alte Pinakothek: 12cra, 30, 31b, 97b.

AWL Images: Stefano Politi Markovina 87t, Christian Mueringer 133.

Bayerische Staatsoper: Wilfried Hösl 75br.

Café Hüller: © SINN-MEDIA 114.

Depositphotos Inc: DaLiu 45t, DmitryRukhlenko 17, Konsultant.gmx.de 13cl, YAY_Images 23b.

Deutsches Museum: 34b, 35t, 35b, 36.

First edition 2005

Published in Great Britain by Dorling
Kindersley Limited, DK, 20 Vauxhall Bridge Road,
London SW1V 2SA

The authorised representative in the EEA is
Dorling Kindersley Verlag GmbH. Arnulfstr.
124, 80636 Munich, Germany

Published in the United States by DK Publishing,
1745 Broadway, 20th Floor, New York, NY 10019, USA

The publishers cannot accept responsibility for any consequences
arising from the use of this book, nor for any material on third
party websites, and cannot guarantee that any website address
in this book will be a suitable source of travel information.

A CIP catalog record for this book
is available from the British Library.

A catalog record for this book is available
from the Library of Congress.

ISSN: 1542 1554
ISBN: 978 0 2417 0950 4

Printed and bound in China

www.dk.com

This book was made with Forest
Stewardship Council™ certified
paper – one small step in DK's
commitment to a sustainable future.
Learn more at **www.dk.com/uk/
information/sustainability**